MINDSET

PROVEN STRATEGIES TO

WITH

BUILD UP YOUR BRAIN,

MUSCLE

BODY AND BUSINESS

JAMIE ALDERTON

R3THINK PRESS

First published in Great Britain 2016
by Rethink Press (www.rethinkpress.com)

CONTENTS

INTRODUCTION

MY STORY

The signs weren't promising. At school I had always had a very short attention span. During my teenage years, I definitely needed guidance and support, as what I mostly enjoyed was alcohol and just not really doing anything productive. In fact, I wouldn't concentrate on anything I didn't want to do, and I'd only really focus on the things that I enjoyed.

I have to say I think this applies to a lot of 'grown ups' today, in that there's a huge disconnect between the things we do on a daily basis and the things that we need to do. So many people are in jobs they hate and spend all day doing things they don't like doing. This, in turn, is one of the reasons that they don't excel at their jobs: it's really hard to progress with things that you hate doing.

But I had always enjoyed going to the gym, and had been going during my lunch hour since the age of thirteen. This was probably the best thing for a kid as hyperactive and as easily bored as me, enabling me to channel some of my surplus energy and to focus on something other than getting into trouble.

Going into the Army had also crossed my mind, but it wasn't until I was seventeen that I thought that unless I made a commitment to it, I was probably going to end up in prison sometime in the next few years, so joining up became something of a no-brainer.

I found I enjoyed Army life. It was pretty straightforward: look after your kit and it will look after you! Preparation is the key to success, so you need to make sure that you are aware of what's going on and have everything for the job in hand with you at all times. If someone tells you to do something, you don't argue, you just get it done (I am the polar opposite of that now, as I hate being told what to do). All in all, I felt I had a purpose in life, and I was proud to be a soldier. I was part of something important, and I was always as pleased as Punch to tell people about my career choice.

I gained a wide range of skills in the Army, qualifying as a communications expert on long and short-range radio equipment and ground-to-air radio communications with helicopters. I had always prided myself on being the best soldier − fit as a fiddle, kit always immaculate: a hard-working individual who always used to impress his peers. What a change from the shiftless teenager I had once been!

As the years went by, though, I started to feel there was more to life than the Army. It was great being part of some-thing bigger than myself, but I was becoming more and more unimpressed with the whole experience: not having a voice of my own and being controlled by power-hungry senior ranks! I had always said to myself that as soon as I stopped enjoying it I would leave, and at around the age of twenty-three, I gave in my year's notice, excited at the prospect of moving on to pastures new.

A NEW START

Leaving the Army began a period of soul-searching. Having spent seven years in the Army, being told what to do and getting on with doing it was kind of ingrained in me. Now there was no longer a sergeant shouting down my neck I needed some focus and some goals. Yet I didn't really know what I wanted to do, and no immediate career prospects beckoned, so when the owner of my gym approached me and suggested I have a go at body-building, I jumped at the opportunity. At last I'd found something that really started to float my boat. Here was the imaginary sergeant I needed, telling me to cook healthy meals, hit the gym and prepare for a contest. It was this structure that gave me vision and focus in life.

I had a great first year competing: I did three shows, coming second in one and winning the British amateur title in another. To say that I took to it like a duck to water would be an understatement. It was so easy for me to adapt what I had learnt in the military to support my competition career just by having a plan of action.

I gave up competition a year later as I was offered a fantastic opportunity to do some contract work in the Middle East, Kenya and Somalia. It was well-paid work in security and administration, and the prospect of exploring more of the world and experiencing different cultures and communities made up for the fact that I would no longer be able to commit to competitions. So this was my life for almost a year, but though I loved the travel and the income, I felt there was something lacking in my life, as I knew I couldn't keep on doing it forever.

Then something happened! I landed in Nairobi one day and headed into the office, where I received a call from my boss at head office in London. They had been making some budget cuts and removing some of the 'non-essential' staff from the projects they were on: unfortunately my services were no longer required... The first thing that came into my head was, 'Couldn't you have told me this nine hours ago, when I was still in London?'

The second thing that came into my head was that I had just put all my savings from the contract job towards a very nice three-storey house so there was nothing left. I remember going back to the UK wondering what on earth I was going to do for a job, as, seriously, I didn't have a clue.

I must have applied for, and been interviewed for, at least ten different jobs in the two weeks after I returned to London. Each time I was unsuccessful, and it was really starting to get me down. I remember sitting on the bed waiting for a phone call from one particular employer about a job as manager of a steelworks, and it was between me and another guy. The phone rang: the other guy had got the job.

I put the phone down, and carried on sitting on my bed, racking my brains about what I should do. Then I started doing something I had never really done before! My brain was so clogged up with ideas and questions that I decided to grab a pen and paper and write stuff down.

I started to write down the stuff that I was good at, the things that I enjoyed and the things that I could be really good at. Then I realised the answer to my problem was just staring me in the face. I loved my training, nutrition and workouts, and I loved helping people. Obviously I should become a personal trainer!

But there was another big problem: I had no money. I did have a credit card, however... . I decided that if I was going to do this there would be no half measures. I would commit totally and work my ass off to make happen whatever needed to happen. I stuck the fees for the personal training certification course onto my card and completed it. I began renting a studio local to my house and filled it with gym equipment, again putting everything on my credit card.

Now I had a studio, a business, and a vision, and I started to get to work. I had always wanted to train clients somewhat differently from the way I had seen other people doing it. None of the trainers I had seen ever really covered any elements outside the weights room, such as diet and mindset, so this was something I really started to focus on with my clients. It was all well and good, them putting in that hour in the gym, but what were they doing with the other twenty-three hours? I made it my mission to go above and beyond the usual service with my clients.

I attracted my first clients by advertising my services on social media – putting it all out there: my studio, my exercise regime, my diet. I would even travel up to London to 'meet' my clients: I'd sit in a café in Oxford Street every Saturday morning to do diet consultations as it had free Wi-Fi.

But there was one thing I realised that I missed, and that was competing. This is why, back in 2012, not only was I working hard to get the new business off the ground, but I was also committed to getting back on stage to compete in the European Championships in Iceland at the end of the year. I gave myself twelve weeks to get ready, working intensively both on my physique and on my business. The hard work and sacrifice paid off: I won the European championships and became a professional competitor.

Then something strange happened: my business went through the roof and I acquired a book full of clients! I thought this was to do with my now being a professional competitor, but it wasn't. It was because I had documented my entire journey to the stage during my twelve weeks of preparation. People were interested in me as a person, not just in the products that I was selling.

And that's when my business really started to change. I understood that I could reach and inspire so many more people just by being me and telling it like it is – not necessarily telling them what to do, but rather showing them what I do, so that they could see that if they took these activities on board and practised them every day, they too would be able to see the benefits.

This has transformed my business over the past few years, and, to be honest, it's transformed me as well. I used to put in front of people only what I thought they wanted to see, and gave away very little about my own life. In effect, people only saw the tip of the iceberg and didn't realise that this success came from everything that was going on below the waterline.

This was a very strange period in the development of my business, because there weren't many people doing what I did – being open and honest and telling the unvarnished truth. However, that all changed in the second year of my business, when Gary Vaynerchuk came into my life. Gary had built two multi-million dollar businesses, and had done so through integrity and hard work. What really inspired me about him was his no-bullshit attitude and his brutal honesty – rare qualities in a world of smoke and mirrors.

The more I put my life and my business on show, the more interest built up, and the comments I was getting were really refreshing. I started to use social media more and more not only to promote myself, but to build my business and reach more people. I started doing more video; I discovered that I really enjoyed talking on camera, so I increased the amount I was doing every day.

People responded well to my no-nonsense attitude, and they began to realise that you could be busy, run your businesses, and still get the results you want at the gym, as long as you work hard and stay consistent. The message I have always stressed is that you should know your strengths and capitalise on them, and know your weaknesses and find ways to turn them into strengths, either by hiring people who excel in those areas to fill these gaps or by working twice as hard on them till they are no longer weaknesses.

I branched out, focusing on nutrition and training, writing my own plans to show people what they could achieve – and transforming thousands of my clients in the process. I also started listening to podcasts and realised the mental benefit from listening to and absorbing the information to be had. I just knew I had to create my own podcast, which I did, and it became the No. 1 Health podcast in the UK. Then, about three years ago, I really started getting into books, and this, too, has transformed my business and my life.

All this has brought me to where I am today with my business, and explains why I felt compelled to write *Mindset with Muscle*.

TRANSFORMING YOURSELF AND YOUR MINDSET

This book is a transformation plan for your success. The way I have structured and written this book is designed to make it action-focused: the whole point is to get you to *do* the exercises and activities that will bring about change in your life.

As I see it, there is a huge problem with the way people handle information in our society. They buy the books, read the magazines, and watch the 'how to' videos, but they fail to put into practice any of the things they have learnt. I know so many people who have read exactly the same books as me, but they haven't improved their lives, increased their fitness or grown their businesses. It's all well and good knowing what to do, but there's actually little point in knowing it unless you do something about it.

What's different about this book is that at the end of every chapter I summarise the key points you need to take away from it and the actions you need to take – and ask you to tweet me once you have completed the actions. This will ensure not only that you are implementing the right things, but that there is also a mechanism for you to hold yourself accountable for getting things done!

There are a number of ways in which people go wrong with their reading:

> They read the material from the author's point of view, rather than considering how it applies to their own lives.

> They don't teach or tell others what they have learnt, which is a fantastic way to help you re-call information.

> They don't act on the information that they read.

> They don't build any accountability into acting on what they've read by setting deadlines for partic-ular tasks or activities.

To make sure that you can read this book constructively and get results from it, it's going to follow a very logical plan.

1. Together we'll start at the beginning, by getting you to define what the problem is before you rush off and start trying to fix it.

2. Then we'll break down the things you need to acknowledge and understand in order to begin to change, and to progress in your transformation.

3. Finally, we'll start to change your way of thinking, so that you become someone who takes action, and holds themselves responsible for the actions that they take.

Is this going to be a perfect process? Hell, no! Our habits and routines come and go, and take many years to evolve. As human beings we change our minds – and our lives – all the time, and what's relevant to us now may no longer be so in a few months' time. But it's vital to understand that this is OK, and that there is a difference between failing and failure, as one of the lists I wrote for myself sums up:

FAILING	FAILURE
> Part of the process	> Given up
> Helps with experience	> Accepted defeat
> Gives you feedback	> Negative Mindset
> Helps you to grow	> Doesn't help you grow
> Helps you learn more	> Your learn nothing

We learn by making mistakes because we learn what not to do. But we can learn a lot quicker from other people's mistakes, since we don't need to repeat them ourselves. This is what I want this book to be about: showing you the path to the success by revealing to you my own path to success via failing.

CHAPTER 1

DEFINING THE PROBLEM

Did you know that our brains produce as many as 50,000 thoughts a day? (This is an average of men's 40,000 thoughts and women's 60,000!) Now, I want you to think about the kinds of things you think about each day. Mostly, it's probably what to wear, what to eat, what to listen to, and so on. But with 50,000 thoughts flying around in your head every day, it can be difficult to focus on which of them are actually going to make a difference in your life. There's a risk that the ones we choose to focus on will not actually benefit us in any way.

We are used to thinking our way through problems, and finding solutions, but how often do we question our thought processes, why we think the way we do, and whether the solutions we choose from our multitude of thoughts are the right ones?

WHAT DO YOU REALLY WANT?

Take the example of someone who is overweight. They will be driven to find a solution to the problem by thinking it through, and it's likely that their thoughts will focus on what they eat, and mechanisms for shedding the weight. To help them do that, they may look to buy some sort of guide to the best solution from a bookshop or off the internet, in the hope that that will be the answer to their problem – but nine times out of ten, it isn't!

This is because they are looking for a solution without having understood the problem. Their problem isn't that they need to lose 20 lbs; their problem is that they don't know why they are 20 lbs overweight. And this is where the hard work really starts: with 50,000 thoughts to sift through every day, it's hard for anyone to pinpoint why they've got to where they are now.

We are the best liars in the world when it comes to our own thoughts and choices – after all, we are the only people we need to convince about whether a particular course of action is right or wrong, and we're inclined to believe ourselves.

If people were really honest with themselves, they'd realise that they're actually looking for a solution to their problems that doesn't involve much change, that allows them to keep their current bad habits and routines, and still achieve the results they're after. It can't be done!

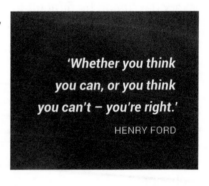

'Whether you think you can, or you think you can't – you're right.'

HENRY FORD

Your problem starts with being honest with yourself. You are where you are today as a result of the decisions that you have made about yourself and the way you live. You can lay the blame on others ('my parents were both over-weight'), and you can talk about how tough it's been for you in the hope that people will understand and empathise, but if you think you're the only one with that particular problem out of a world population of 7.1 billion people, then you are sadly mistaken.

So what you also need to realise is that there are thousands if not millions of people out there with the same problem as you, some of whom choose to accept it and some of whom don't. Just because you haven't met them doesn't mean that they don't exist!

At the heart of your problem, though, is that what you want actually goes beyond what you think you want. When I ask them why they want to be slimmer, a lot of people say 'I'll feel better.' When I ask clients what they mean by that, it's usually that they feel they'd have more energy, focus and confidence. My answer to that is that they need to focus on being that person now. Reducing their gravitational pull to the earth will not on its own change their brains.

The confidence that apparently comes from being slimmer is in effect a by-product, not of being slimmer, but of having set a goal, planned how to go about achieving it, and having succeeded in achieving it. Achievers are the most confident people in the world, and the reason they achieve so much is because they break things down into manageable goals, and 'reverse engineer' things – working backwards from where they know they want to be.

Unfortunately, most of us are very impulse-driven. 'I want to be 10lbs lighter,' we say, and we're off. This enthusiasm can be a huge asset, but it only gets you so far. You risk just getting your head down and proceeding off down any old path. I know this, because it's exactly what I did myself. I went off down the wrong path all the time, but I didn't stop. Then I found a new path, and I went down that one, but it turned out to be wrong, so I went down another one, and so on. It was only because the army had disciplined me not to give up that I persisted until I found the right path. But not everyone has been trained in this way, so it's better if they have a good understanding of the problem, and of how they may have been failing to resolve it before, and a detailed plan of action – a route map – to keep them on track.

Bear in mind that if you are reading this book, you probably have the luxury of having a roof over your head and food in the fridge. This means that you almost certainly have enough control over your own life to make decisions about it and to act on them.

For a start, one of the 50,000 thoughts running through your head was the decision to buy this book. Other decisions from this teeming pool of thoughts will have governed whether you exercised today, and how well you ate. These choices are being offered to you constantly; all you need to do is to understand them better so that you can change your life.

And it all starts with writing them down!

WRITING IT ALL DOWN

Be honest: what was the last thing you wrote down? A shopping list? You knew what you needed, your list gave you a plan of action, and once you went to the supermarket you were able to tick off the items as you put them into your basket. Writing things down is one of the easiest things that people can do, and yet it is a vastly underused resource.

It's like any other activity: you have to build up a habit of writing, incorporating it into your routine. There are different ways to write things down, and different reasons for doing so:

> ❯ articulating feelings;

> ❯ defining goals;

> ❯ setting out problems;

> ❯ working out solutions; and

> ❯ clearing your head!

The first time I wrote down something that had a major impact on my life was when I was made redundant; and I did it because I had been left with no choice but to try to figure out what to do next.

What writing things down showed me very clearly was that I had not been honest with myself about what I wanted in life. When I left the Army, we were given what are called Enhanced Learning Credits – in effect, several thousand pounds to help you choose and train for a new career outside the military. I wasted those credits! The course I chose and the career path I opted to go down were based on one thing only: money!

I was looking at the highest-paid jobs and focused on getting qualified to do them, on the assumption that earning the amounts of money these jobs brought in would make me happy. But there was a problem: the qualifications and the jobs were well out of my comfort zone, and I really struggled to master the knowledge that I would need in order to get a job in that industry. Advanced IT networks were just not for me!

I nearly made the same mistake again when I was made redundant from my post-army consultancy work. I searched for the jobs with the highest pay, and if I had found one what would have happened next? I certainly wouldn't have found the real solution to my problem.

Now that I began to write things down, the solution to my problem was staring me in the face:

I love fitness; I love training; I love helping people.

I SHOULD BE A PERSONAL TRAINER!

Once I had written this down, I started to write everything down: everything to do with fitness, my feelings, business, and, well, life. And that's when my world started to change.

I became more honest with myself about what it was that I actually wanted to do. Writing cleared my head of all the confusion, and helped me to identify the things I really needed to do, and those I didn't need to do.

THE USE OF WRITING TO PLAN

One of the biggest things I've learnt from writing things down is how to be more productive when you are apparently 'busy'. The problem with busy people is that they are always busy and they have a lot of things to get done in a day. But what makes them even busier than they need to be is that they fail to plan out their day and allocate time for the tasks that they need to achieve. Half the time they are so busy thinking about all the things they need to get done that they don't actually do any of them: the classic 'paralysis by analysis'.

When they write things down, though, they realise that they're not as busy as they thought they were, or they are busy, but they're less stressed because now they know that all their tasks have been allocated some time.

Writing down your day also enables you to allocate time not only for tasks you need to achieve, but for activities that you enjoy. Here is a typical day for me, as written down.

5:45am	wake up
6am - 7:15am	power walk (listening to an audio book or podcasts)
7:15am - 7:30am	mapping out my day in my diary
7:30am - 7:45am	social media posts
7:45am - 8:15am	breakfast and YouTube videos
8:45am - 10:45am	gym
11am - 12pm	Skype meetings
12pm - 12:30pm	lunch and YouTube video
12:30pm - 2pm	emails and social media posts
2pm - 2:30pm	reading for 30 minutes
2:30pm - 4:30pm	podcast guest, emails and social media
4:40pm - 6:30pm	time with my daughter Elyza
6:30pm - 8pm	catch-ups and emails plus social media
8pm - 9pm	dinner and TV
9pm - 10pm	one episode of a TV series
10:30pm	bed

As you can see, I've allocated time for everything that needs to be done, but I've also factored in time for things I enjoy doing, like reading and spending time with my daughter. Because those things are on my list, doing them also feels like an achievement, even though they are non-work activities that I really enjoy and that benefit all the family. In effect, I'm setting myself up to win by ensuring that I build in activities that help me to deal with stress. You can't be productive if you're stressed, which means that the positive knock-on effects of planning out your day are phenomenal.

WRITING AS A VALUABLE REFERENCE

What you've written down can be a lasting and valuable resource. If I remember that I've come across a particular problem before, I can look back to see what I did to resolve it previously. Similarly, when I'm training for a competition, I log my weight every single day and record what I've eaten and the amount of exercise I've taken, and I draw on this information the next time I am preparing for an event. Whether you keep a physical journal or a digital journal, having that data to hand is so important.

Over the longer term, journaling and writing things down can offer you concrete proof of the progress you've made. If you feel you've come to a bit of a standstill, you need only look back at what you have documented over previous years and months to see what you have achieved, and the boost you get from that will motivate you to persevere.

I see this a lot in the context of weight loss. People come to me and say, ' I'm still overweight' or 'I'm still a stone away from my goal', and I have to point out to them that they've already lost two stone and remind them – with a picture – of where they started from. They're often genuinely surprised, as they've forgotten what they were like six months previously. It really fires them up to continue with their plans.

ADDING VALUE

As well as writing, I've done a lot of listening, and it was through this that I gained the insight that whether the problem was weight loss, or fitness, or building a business, you needed to have a well-rounded (as opposed to a narrow) understanding of it. My view is that this is what happens when you turn your hobby and your passion into a business: you go the extra mile without even being aware that you're doing so.

I like talking as well as listening, so I've never been backwards in pointing out to people where they are going wrong, and what they could do to remedy it. It never occurred to me at first to turn this into a business. Although I was often brutally honest with my clients at the gym, they trusted me. I might not have had the sports science degree, but I had immense practical experience, and I drew on that, rather than on textbooks, to advise them.

What's more, people are motivated by seeing what someone who is just like them can achieve. I go down the pub, I'd been to the same sort of schools as a lot of my clients – I am a normal person. Just add a good work ethic and a consistent approach and you too can achieve your goals. That was a very engaging message for clients and potential clients, and if people believe what you say they will be prepared to buy what you sell.

I now sell a lot of different products, but most of them are based on asking people the right questions (not least, 'What are you struggling with?'), and then creating a product that provides a solution, rather than sitting in a bubble thinking up things I could offer and planning how to market them. I worked this out for myself, and, as with so many things, it was not until a lot later that I came across the books that endorse this approach.

In fact, I see this a lot in business. I see people doing great things and they've never read a business book in their lives. The reason that they're so successful is because they're just good people. They genuinely care about others and want good things for them, which in turn helps grow their business because they're nice people to be around. They make you happy, and they inspire and motivate you.

I'd contrast that approach with much of what goes on in the fitness industry, where people are just focused on trying to find very, very key minimal things that they can do to get results: 'If you eat this food, you will lose weight', 'If you train this particular way, you will lose weight', which may get very short-term results, but unless you're focusing on your habits, your routines and the way that you live your life, you're not going to have a sustainable transformation.

THE LONG GAME

The discipline required when it comes to nutrition and training for competition is exactly like that required for building a business. A lot of it just comes down to sticking to the principles and the plan, and being consistent. No successful business has become successful overnight. It's taken many, many hours and many, many months and years of consistent habits, of doing the same productive activities over and over again.

A lot of people like to try and make it all sexy, full of variety and fun. The reality is that a lot of it isn't. Most businesses are built on consistency, on being able to provide the same level of service or quality of product, day in, day out. It's repetition, exactly the same as nutrition and training. Unfortunately, people get very bored very easily, which is something that I try to focus on with them. They need to realise that most of the time it's a case of just turning up and doing it every day, and not thinking, 'How much longer have I got of this?'

In my own case, I simply applied to my business the same principles I had adopted with my nutrition and training. Just as I log my food intake, I log the people I've spoken to and their particular interests, I log emails, identify follow-ups to pursue, and I build a strategy from all this. If you have a passion for your business, these habits and routines will never be tiresome or oppressive for you.

CONTEXT

One of the most important elements of your potential to solve your problems and develop a resilient and constructive mindset is the context that you are operating in. Personally, I have been fortunate in having the self-discipline that the army instilled into me to support me in developing both my fitness regime and my business. Most people don't have that, so instead they need ideally to be in an environment that makes it easy to keep to consistent habits and to put in the work required.

This doesn't mean, for example, that you can never go out for a drink with friends. You just have to maintain a determined mindset when you do so! My own informal research in this area has confirmed that this pays off. Occasionally, I do go to bars with the lads, and sooner or later, after a few drinks, they get the shots in. I always turn shots down, and they always turn to me and say, 'Go on, Jay, just one shot!' It's a herd mentality, but I never give into that peer pressure, however much they take the mickey out of me. What I do is wait ten minutes, and then turn to the person who was egging me on the most energetically and ask 'Are you still annoyed with me for not having a shot?' Often as not, they'll ask me what I'm on about, because although it seemed like the most important thing at the time, now they really don't care.

But beware of surrounding yourself only with successful people, because that won't necessarily enable you to empathise and understand other people's situations. It's hard to overstate how important it is to engage with people, to understand where they're coming from and how you will be able to help them (and don't assume you will be able to help everybody). You're bound to come across people with a very negative mindset, and although you might not want to spend a great deal of time in their company, you owe it to yourself and them to gain insight into why they are like this and what you can draw from it.

But before we move on to creating the right context through adapting your habits and routines, here's a summary and your challenge for this chapter.

SUMMARY

Make sure you define your problem accurately; dig deep and don't just accept it at face value. What's really going on?

Write things down; it's the foundation for reflection, planning, analysis and tracking your progress.

Make what you have to offer people genuine and personal, find out their needs, and above all be consistent.

Make things easier for yourself by seeking out like-minded colleagues and companions, but engage with and listen to all your contacts: everyone has something to teach you.

CHALLENGE

- Get up half an hour earlier, go for a walk, and think about your situation.

- Once you have thought about it, write down what you're not happy about.

- What are you going to do about it?

- What you need to do now is tweet me @GrenadeJay to tell me what you're going to do about it – instant accountability!

CHAPTER 2

HABITS AND ROUTINES

Every day we build habits in our brains. Some are good and have a positive impact on our lives; some of them are bad and have a negative impact. You need a routine in order to build a habit, so without a routine you will find it hard to develop any new habits you want to acquire. In fact, it's hard to maintain a routine without forming habits.

But that's not all you need. Take going to the gym, for example: you can set up a routine that enables you to go to the gym three times a week by pencilling it into your diary and making sure you go there, but that doesn't mean that you will either continue to do it, or actually enjoy doing it.

What makes habits so important when it comes to fitness is, of course, that they are repeated regularly, and what's more, they start to happen subconsciously. When is the last time that you consciously thought, 'mirror, signal, manoeuvre' when you were driving? Wouldn't it be great if your health and fitness habits were like that? What if you subconsciously reached for the right foods and exercised every day without any effort? Well, I'm telling you it's possible, as this is what I now do myself.

In the first chapter we talked about defining the problem, and the most common problem is usually to do with the current bad habits that people have in their lives. If you can start to build a routine based on good habits, you will find that as you begin to feel better and maybe lose weight, you will become more motivated to keep to it, and the habits of eating healthily and exercising will become easier.

BREAKING BAD HABITS

A bad habit can be very difficult to get rid of, especially if you have had it for a number of years. Ingrained, daily habits are usually performed subconsciously, so that most of the time you are not even aware that you are doing them.

Take the habit of biting your nails, which is a common one. The solution is often to paint your fingers with a bitter-tasting liquid. You only realise how often you've been doing this when you find yourself with a horrible taste in your mouth several times an hour!

What the bitter solution does is to act as a trigger: you begin to associate biting your nails with this horrible taste, and this provides a powerful motivation for you to stop. This is a useful way to look at bad habits and think about what would motivate you to stop them. Some people have even been known to give their friends money to look after which must be paid over to a cause they actively oppose if they don't keep up their exercise targets!

Bad habits can stand in the way of making changes in many ways. Physically, eating too little and exercising too much can be just as damaging as the opposite. Bad mental habits such as constant self-criticism and always focusing on the negative aspects of any situation make it much harder to improve your routines and your environment (see Chapter 3).

What I'm not saying is that you've got to go out and give up everything. The simple logic of 'reduce or remove' is a much better recipe for success — reduce the habit, but if you find you can't then remove it completely. But try reduction first — people sometimes find that the minute something is banned they end up wanting it more than they ever did in the first place! Tackling bad habits one at a time by this method is far more effective.

I still indulge in a few bad habits on a weekly basis: I'm prepared to admit that my love for Skittles and vodka probably doesn't help me with my overall fitness goals, but as in general my healthy living habits by far exceed these two bad ones, there's not too much damage done.

CREATING NEW HABITS

Patience is the key when it comes to creating new habits. The problem is often that people are very, very impatient, but habit change isn't something that happens in a couple of weeks. You are looking at something like sixty-five to seventy days — in

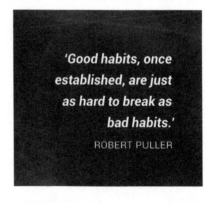

'*Good habits, once established, are just as hard to break as bad habits.*'
ROBERT PULLER

succession — of performing a new action before it starts to become more of a subconscious habit.

What we need to do is exploit our triggers. Every day we have hundreds of triggers that remind us to do things: these triggers have been shaped by the routines and rituals that we have adopted over the years. A morning sequence of triggers might go like this:

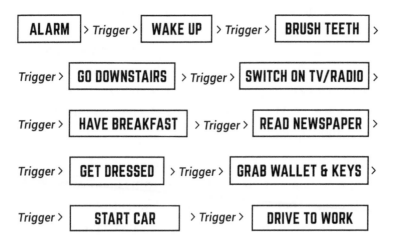

You can create reminders for new habits by 'pinning' them to your current daily habits. I like to call this 'habit hacking'. All you need to do is to make a list of a number of things that you do every day without even thinking about it. Here is part of my list to get you started:

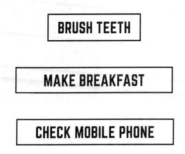

Any of these activities will be a great place to start a new habit and this is how to do it.

Starting My New Habit

In front of where I stand to brush my teeth, I put a note on the wall that read 'What are the three things that you are grateful for today?' Now what happened is every time I brushed my teeth I saw this simple reminder and I thought about three things I felt thankful for. It was often my job, my daughter, or something that was going really well in my life – perhaps training.

Within a few weeks I no longer needed the note to remind me to think about these three things as I had become conditioned to associate doing this with brushing my teeth. This new habit has enabled me to increase my daily happiness first thing in the morning, which in turn helps me to have a more positive and productive day. And it all started with a little note by my toothbrush.

This is a pretty simple new habit, though, and not all habits are as easy to create. It can be much harder to adopt a more challenging habit, such as exercising regularly. With a habit that is more difficult to adopt, you have to understand how habits are formed and make them easier. The diagram below sums up this cycle.

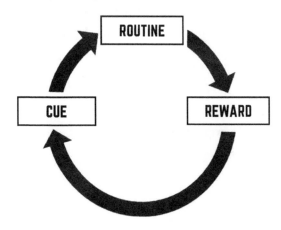

In his book, *The Power of Habit*, Charles Duhigg explained in detail the process involved in abandoning an old habit and adopting a new one.

Everyone has their own cues or triggers for particular habits. Sitting down in front of the television after work can be the cue for people to overeat, dipping into snacks without really being aware of how much they are eating, or to crack open a few beers, which would certainly stand in the way of your fitness goals. If you can understand your own triggers you have a better chance of controlling them.

The routine is the action you are performing at the time when you are practising your habit. The reward is the pleasure you get from your habit: aren't Pringles wonderful? What's not to like about a cold beer? This pleasure reinforces your behaviour: having a beer makes you feel good; biting your nails makes you feel less stressed. Once you start to analyse what your rewards are and write them down, you can work out ways to adapt your routines so they don't trigger bad habits and in fact become the basis of good habits. You will need to do a bit of experimentation to make it work for you. Could you sit down in front of the television after your meal, so you won't be hungry enough to snack? Or could you have some healthy superfood snacks to hand instead of snacks filled with crap?

Here are two routines that entail good habits – habits that have a positive impact on my life when it comes to keeping in shape and feeling good.

MORNING ROUTINE

| CUE | my alarm goes off

| HABIT | switch off alarm, get my clothes on, and go out for my power walk

| REWARD | feel fired up for the rest of the day because I have had exercise and time to think

I have made this habit so much easier by doing what I call 'setting yourself up to win'. Before I go to bed I lay my walking clothes out ready for the morning. I also download an audio book or a podcast that I really want to listen to, as this adds to the positive triggers. I put my trainers out ready by the door, and make sure my headphones, water and morning supplements are ready in their usual place so I can just grab them.

All this means that when I wake up I can just get up and go, and it stops me from creating some excuse in my head, turning over and going back to sleep.

COOKING ROUTINE

| CUE | mealtime

| HABIT | get scales out and log on to my phone calorie counter

| REWARD | healthy food that I enjoy, but that has been measured and managed in line with my goals.

I had a friend over and at breakfast time he saw me following my routine of getting my scales out and logging onto my calorie counter while I was talking to him. My friend doesn't really exercise much, nor does he really care about what he eats, and he said to me, 'Do you always weigh your food?' I looked at the scales and I looked at him, and said 'I guess I do.'

What was fascinating to me is that I have obviously been doing this for so many years that I actually do it almost unconsciously, without even thinking about it. Most people wouldn't consider this 'normal', but for me food preparation is the trigger to weigh my food. This habit, however, has ensured that I've hit all my calorie and macronutrient targets without having to think about it too much.

COMMON MISTAKES

CHANGING TOO MUCH AT ONCE

This happens a lot! You decide that it's time you got yourself into shape and what do you do? You try to change all your habits at once:

You go to the gym four to five times a week when you've never been before.

You start eating foods that you don't normally eat, or even like!

You stop socialising with your friends.

All in all, you spend too much time trying to get into shape and not enough time with your family.

This is far too much for your brain to take on all in one go. You might be able to keep it up for a few weeks, but eventually the new regime will begin to slide and you'll find yourself back in your old habits.

Such false starts are all too common with people trying to lose weight, as they are suddenly emotionally connected to the effort they are making, and they are looking for a quick fix. The reality is that there are no quick fixes, and this is the flaw in a lot of the extreme diets and exercise regimes that are out there. If you follow the system you will get the results, but these plans do not train you in new habits; they just teach you to follow a singular course of action and for this reason are doomed to failure.

Most people are really only able to commit to one or two big habit changes at a time. It takes so long to turn a new action into a habit and incorporate it into a routine that you need to choose changes that you can put into practice consistently.

KEEP IT SIMPLE

A lot of people look for the secrets of success in absolutely everything they do. They want to get results fast, change their lives, etc., etc. – and that's precisely their problem! When you overcomplicate things, not only do you end up feeling inadequate or unmotivated, but you actually get far worse results.

I could write the most effective nutrition plan in the world for a client – one that made sure they hit all their macro-nutrient targets for the day; achieved the ideal balance between protein, fats and carbs for their goals; and gave them the perfect calorie range for the best possible fat loss – but if what I gave them was not enjoyable, maintainable, and something they can still be doing a year from now, then despite the effectiveness of the plan it would not be the right one for them and I would have been wasting their time and mine.

If you start off by understanding your current good and bad habits, identifying which ones might need a little tweak here and there, changing things a little at a time through tiny steps, then your plan will yield better results than one which is more rigorous and demanding.

BAD FOR BUSINESS

Not understanding consumer habits can be bad for the profits and growth of a business, especially when it comes to service-based offerings and solutions. Too many businesses focus on trying to give the customer everything. This sounds to them like a fantastic plan, because if the customer has everything they need, they have no reason to look elsewhere.

There's a phrase that a lot of information and communication businesses swear by, which is, 'Content is King'. To me that is simply wrong. The phrase should be, 'Usability of content is King'! Of course it's important to have great content, but if there is too much of it people are just overwhelmed, they switch off, and then they don't achieve anything (paralysis by analysis again).

This is all down to the way our brains work, as I'm going to demonstrate now with a little thought experiment.

Suppose I asked you for recommendations for three songs for me to play in the car right now, you have ten seconds to do it in, and ready, steady, go … The chances are that you would struggle just to blurt out three songs as you would have been spoilt for choice. Now say I asked you a more specific question: recommendations for three Michael Jackson songs in ten seconds. This will be lot easier as I've cut down the options and reduced the stress.

If you make things simpler, give people less choice (does, 'You can have any colour you like, as long as it's black' ring any bells?), and focus on one or two key components, the consumer will not only be able to achieve more of what they intended, but they will get into the habit of using the information that you are offering a lot more quickly.

You have only to look at the sparseness of Amazon's checkout page. The average person has only a seven second memory span when they're online, and Amazon doesn't want to distract them in any way from making a payment!

So whether it's weight loss or business milestones you are trying to achieve, don't overcomplicate things: concentrate on the one or two factors that will really make a difference.

KEEP ON KEEPING ON

What a lot of people do is to set unrealistic goals for themselves, creating a lot of unnecessary pressure. Take dieting, for example. People tell themselves that they're not going to eat this, and they're not going to eat that, and then they go out and get carried away and end up eating precisely what they promised themselves they wouldn't. Then they despair, think they've failed completely and give up.

What they fail to realise is that one slice of chocolate cake is not going to impede your progress towards your goals, any more than one missed workout will. If you overdo the calories on one day, remember it's just one day. You can reduce your calorie intake slightly over the next few days so that by the end of the week you will be hitting the same target as if you had not eaten the cake.

Another reason that people give up too soon is that they don't recognise how far they've come. Someone might be distressed to find themselves still ten pounds off their target weight, completely overlooking the fact that they are now twenty pounds lighter than they were six months ago – surely a cause for celebration and keeping up the good work rather than giving up.

PROGRESS ABOVE PERFECTION

We spend a lot of time searching for the perfect body, the perfect job, and the perfect business, but so often our concept of what is perfect is based on what other people are thinking and doing. It's all too easy to look at someone else's life and think how much better yours would be if, say, you had a body like them. The fact is you are not like them. In the unlikely event that I was able to cut off your head and stick it on their body, you would find that you couldn't sustain that body for very long because you are not that person and you don't have their habits and mindset. The same applies in business and in life.

How you perceive the world is unique to you, so in making changes you need to consider your habits and your goals. My habits and routines are based on my current goals, and it's important for me, as a body-building competitor, to keep progressing in the gym, and raising the bar with my nutrition and training. It would be pointless to adopt my goals and routines if, as are most people, you are only aspiring to be leaner and have visible abs on the beach!

If this is your goal, then trying to be perfect in what you are doing day by day is the worst thing you can do. If you have a lot of weight to lose, then guess what? It's going to take a long time, so that's why it's a good idea to focus on your existing routines and habits. That way it will be a lot easier to make your positive changes as automatic as possible.

SUMMARY

You will be much more successful in your progress towards your goals if you can turn conscious actions into subconscious habits.

Don't try to do too much at once: make small changes, and as these become habits you can move on to new things.

You are aiming for progress, not perfection. Don't let one cream cake or missed training session derail you.

Beware of too much choice.

CHALLENGE

- Identify one bad habit you'd like to get rid of.
- Identify one good habit you'd like to adopt.
- Tweet me at @grenadejay and let me know your plans!

CHAPTER 3

CONTROLLING YOUR ENVIRONMENT

How Your Environment Shapes You

> *'Environment dictates performance'*
>
> CALLUM LAING, CEO of unique business development organisation Growth Accelerator

This is one of my favourite quotations, because it's just so true. The environment you choose for yourself will either help you or hinder you in reaching your goals. To understand your environment better and to control it better, you need to know that the way you view your world is based on two things:

> your life experiences to date, and

> your current perception of the world.

YOUR LIFE EXPERIENCES

What you have lived through so far will dictate your view of your life and of the world around you. I don't believe in talking about the world from the perspective of anyone other than myself – I can't know what is in anyone else's head and it wouldn't be right to try to second-guess it. All I can do is tell you where I'm coming from.

My previous jobs and career choices brought me a very wide range of experiences. Spending a lot of time away from family and friends, often in some extremely stressful situations – when my life was on the line daily – means there is a lot to measure my current life against. The work I do now isn't really stressful at all. I love what I'm doing, and I'm very grateful to be in a position to do it. I'm also not getting shot at or blown up daily, which kind of helps when it comes to stress management!

My career took me to some dangerous places in the Middle East and on the Horn of Africa, in Mogadishu and Somalia. I have these past experiences to thank for my view of the world today, and for my feeling that we should be immensely grateful for what we have.

But I'm also aware that some people have had really terrible experiences that affect their personal lives and relationships, and their current level of performance in their careers. In this situation you can place all the blame on your misfortunes and allow them to hold you back, or you can embrace them as the spur that drives you forward.

YOUR CURRENT PERCEPTION OF THE WORLD

For me, perception is a fundamental element in shaping your mindset.

perception

/pəˈsɛpʃ(ə)n/

noun

1. the ability to see, hear, or become aware of
   something through the senses.
   "the normal limits to human perception"
2. the way in which something is regarded,
   understood, or interpreted.
   "Hollywood's perception of the tastes of the
   American public"

We have five senses that we use every day to interrogate, interpret and understand the world around us: sight, sound, taste, touch and smell. Whatever we absorb through these senses every day has an effect on lives, for good or ill. But what I find amazing is how much you can control what you are taking in through your senses by making a few simple changes to your life.

I want to focus on the senses of sight and sound, as these are the two through which we now gather most information about our world. In an increasingly visual culture we are constantly being bombarded with images in a way that would have been unimaginable fifty years ago.

Our consumption of the media and of social media has to be discriminating, as with food. You know that if you stuff yourself with sugary, crap food it will not do you any favours, and in the same way you have to be discriminating with the information that you are allowing into your mind. Negative social media posts, spiteful gossip in magazines – these won't inspire you to do more with your life, whereas following people on social media whose lives have a purpose will motivate you. Don't underestimate how much a diet of negativity can warp your perception of yourself and your potential, not to mention your perception of those around you and life in general.

The table below summarises what's on offer; it's up to you to choose from the menu.

NEGATIVE	POSITIVE
Listening to/watching the news compulsively	Keeping up with positive news
Listening to negative people	Listening to inspiring and motivational people
Reading newspapers	Reading books that help you with your life
Reading gossip magazines	Finding inspirational quotes and websites
Following negative social media	Following positive people on social media
Watching too much 'empty calorie' TV/films	Watching YouTube videos and programmes that educate and motivate you

Just by looking at the lists above you will see how easy it is to change the things you see and hear every day from negatives into positives, which in turn will help you to create a positive environment around you. It's like the words of the old song, which urges you to accentuate the positive and eliminate the negative.

OTHER MENTAL INFLUENCES

Beyond these very personal factors that shape the way your mind works are the mental influences that affect all of us. First and foremost are the *multiple distractions* that could throw us off course every minute of every day, if we let them. I'm certainly prone to this, so that's why I'll turn off my mobile if I want to have a productive hour or day.

And the fall-out from this situation is *information overload*, leading to paralysis by analysis. Paradoxically, the fact that we have all this information at our fingertips means that we don't know who or what to listen to. The answer in this situation is to FOCUS:

F OLLOW

O NE

C OURSE

U NTIL

S UCCESSFUL

Another factor that might threaten your single-minded pursuit of your goals is the phenomenon of *herd mentality/ groupthink/peer pressure* – it displays itself in many ways and in many contexts.

A typical example of this would be if you were to find yourself in a foreign airport, where you didn't speak the local language, and all of a sudden there was a commotion, with security guards shouting at the tops of their voices. You would probably panic, look around to see what others were doing, and fall in with them. If they started lining up, then you would probably line up with them too.

This works in a far less extreme environment, too. Let's say that in a particular office there is a culture of having doughnuts on a Friday. Everybody gets excited about the doughnuts on a Friday, and the whole office joins in... except you. Since you aren't doing what everyone else is doing, you stand out from the crowd, which not only makes you feel uncomfortable, but it makes the others around you feel uncomfortable as well. As you can see, controlling your environment in a setting where a herd mentality prevails can be very difficult.

A large part of this is because we care so much about what other people think. We hate to be the odd one out, and we hate people to disapprove of our opinions and actions. And yet, the chances are that ten minutes after the last doughnut has disappeared most people will have forgotten that you didn't have one (just as in my story about the shots in Chapter 1).

The most important lesson to learn about the opinions of others is that they really don't matter. The truth is that we are all the stars of our own story and see others around us as merely extras. You may think that a lot of people are looking at you and thinking about you, but actually they are just thinking about themselves and their starring role in their own film!

So how much easier does it make it to turn down that office doughnut when you know how quickly it will be forgotten, leaving you closer to your goals than you would have been if you'd eaten it? The real difference here is to look at this end goal. Your co-workers may not like your doughnut choice, but they sure as hell will be coming to you for advice when they see that what you are currently doing is working! At first they ask you why, then they ask you how.

PHYSICAL INFLUENCES

It's not all just in the mind, however. There are physical influences that we are subject to that cannot be ignored, however much we might like to think that the principle of mind over matter applies.

I've observed personally that when it comes to physical education in schools in the UK and in the USA things are very different. When I was at school we never really took sports too seriously – yes, there was a school sports day and the occasional five-a-side football match, but sport simply wasn't a huge factor in my schooling, and very little of the school budget went on it. But look across the pond to the USA and a lot of schools have their own stadiums, and college football teams have a huge budget and serious programmes of training and development. The USA may have a worse obesity problem than we do, but its athletes, and even its casual gym-goers, seem to be way ahead of the guys and girls that I've seen in the gyms and on the competitive stages around the world. I believe this is the result of having a more disciplined attitude towards exercise and sport from a young age, and therefore training better. My strong, almost subconscious habits and developed physique stem from the fact that I started early.

One has only to look at how Kenyan runners dominate long-distance and endurance running events to see how physical environment dictates performance. I spent eight months in Kenya and I definitely noticed that it was more difficult to walk and hill-run out there, because of the altitude and the thinner air. Add to this the fact that most Kenyans cannot afford their own transport so spend a lot of time commuting on foot and you can see how their environment has trained them up in endurance and in very effective use of the oxygen in their bodies, leading to athletic performance that is hard to match.

SOCIAL INFLUENCES

There is no denying that the surroundings you are born into have a huge impact, and countless studies confirm the damaging effect of cycles of deprivation. But how is it that some people manage to overcome these disadvantages?

Certainly things didn't look promising for me when I started out in life: I barely scraped my GCSEs, I flunked the last year of college, and if I hadn't joined the army who knows where I might have ended up?

Yes, there are many social factors that may make it more difficult for you to achieve what you want to achieve, but if you can learn to spot them and understand them, you can, if you're willing to make the effort, make changes that will cancel them out. I've listed a few below, with some suggestions about how people have managed to break free of the adverse impact these have been having on their lives:

Education and job opportunities: explore volunteering in your area of interest, and be prepared to start small; make the most of online resources and any libraries near you.

Low social aspiration: nowadays you can seek support from an online community if the one that surrounds you geographically is getting in the way of your potential, and there is of course now the scope to find like-minded people in your geographical area through online social networks.

Access to technology: control technology, don't let it control you, but if the problem is lack of access to it, locate places that offer free or cheap access such as libraries or other institutions – see if your local authority has anything to offer.

Access to transport: unaffordability of transport can be very limiting, but if you can get hold of a cheap bike, some councils offer both free riding and maintenance courses – and plenty of walking or cycling will certainly help you meet your fitness goals!

Make these disadvantages spurs to action rather than excuses for inaction.

TAKING ACTION

In the previous chapter I looked at the pitfalls of trying to change too much at once, especially when it comes to radical dieting or trying to launch yourself into punishing exercise regimes. The message is the same when it comes to controlling your environment. I'm definitely not advising that you become some sort of hermit, cut off from contact with others and living just in a little bubble of like-minded athletes or entrepreneurs.

BALANCING THE COMPANY YOU KEEP

We are all pre-conditioned to want to fit in. This means that the pursuit of success and achievement can sometimes leave you a bit of an outcast. Since you usually need to get yourself out of a comfortable environment to achieve things, don't be surprised if no one is willing to follow you down this route. In order to grow a business, you've got to be working two or three times harder than most people are prepared to do; in order to be in great shape, you've got to prioritise your nutrition and training, which most people are not prepared to do.

So you may well find yourself out on your own, but what you need to get across to people that this is not about superiority. Just because you are not doing what they would expect or want you do to do, doesn't mean that you think you are better than them. You have taken a decision about how you want to live, and you are acting on it. You have understood what you need to do to achieve that change, and you are creating the conditions that will allow you to do it. If that means that you are escaping the herd mentality, so be it. It's a decision that's open to anyone to take.

CASE STUDY: JUSTIN

My client Justin is the perfect example of someone controlling his environment not by controlling what he is taking in through his senses, but by dealing effectively with the information he absorbs. Justin worked in IT, and his colleagues were not the healthiest of people. Not surprisingly, when Justin started a transformation plan with me, he received a lot of negative feedback from them. They made fun of the meals he brought in, and gave him a lot of stick for turning down the Friday treats and passing on the celebrations. Justin found this extremely difficult for the first couple of weeks, as it made him feel like a loner, a bit of an outsider. But he just kept on top of his healthy eating regime, six weeks passed and people really started to notice.

He wasn't just keeping up with the regime, he was looking happier and healthier, too. He began to get compliments and people asking him what exactly it was he was doing. Within eight weeks, two or three of his colleagues started to follow some of the routines that Justin had set up, bringing a water bottle and their own prepared food into the office rather than heading down to the cafeteria for lunch.

This illustrates perfectly, 'First they ask you why, and then they ask you how', and how you can change people's mindset without pressuring them to follow you.

It's certainly helpful to belong to a group of people, perhaps at the gym, who share your goals for fitness. But suppose you wanted to take it further, to become a personal trainer or a fitness coach? Of around 1,500 clients that I've worked with, around 10% of them have gone on to become personal trainers themselves. It wouldn't be helpful to cut yourself off completely from the average person's way of thinking. You need to have some insight into how potential clients see the world, because they won't be surrounded by people encouraging them with their fitness goals.

Similarly, as I pointed out in Chapter 2, it's important to have balance in your life and to ensure your quest to achieve your goals, be they fitness goals, or business goals, or any others, doesn't exclude your family.

You can't hope to exclude every element of negativity from your life, and nor should you try to. You can reduce them, and increase the positive elements, tipping the balance in your favour.

FEED YOUR HEAD

There is a paradox in our online world of instant access to information from millions of sources, and that's that it tends to get filtered to suit our preferences. Twenty years ago we would always be coming up against views we didn't agree with or topics we weren't interested in because a limited number of channels on terrestrial television and fairly mainstream printed publications were all we had to choose from. Now, though, countless algorithms calculate our interests and filter what we are offered on line on the basis of these findings.

In one sense, this is terrific. It means we can easily locate the blogs and the YouTube videos that will help us to develop our fitness or give us advice based on practical experience about how to grow our business. This is an important way of controlling our environment: by surrounding ourselves with a supportive community that we can look to for encouragement and inspiration.

But just as it's unhelpful to adopt an all-or-nothing perspective on your fitness ('I ate a cream cake: there's no point in carrying on!'), it's not helpful to exclude everything that does not fit in with your specific interests and aspirations. If you are someone who will not accept any element of negativity, who insists on living in some cloud-cuckoo land of sweetness and light, the effect on you when you are inescapably confronted with something that doesn't fit in with your world view is going to be far more devastating than if you had acknowledged and managed negative influences as part of your normal coping strategies.

CASE STUDY: CHANGING YOUR THINKING

My client John was finding it very hard to get results, because not only was he surrounded by very negative people, he was also listening to and reading the wrong advice. He would buy any fitness magazine he could lay his hands on and write out lots of different workouts and routines for himself. All he ended up with was conflicting information, which got him nowhere when it came to reaching his fitness goals. I asked him to spend less time with the negative people, to focus on surrounding himself with more like-minded people – and to stop buying endless quantities of fitness magazines but to concentrate on the fitness activities he liked doing. John found a circle of fellow fitness enthusiasts, which helped him to stay on track and change his mindset to a more positive one. He was able to simplify his training and nutrition and focus (**Follow One Course Until Successful**) on doing the things he actually wanted to do, and as a result he achieved an amazing transformation in the six months that I worked with him.

ACCENTUATE THE POSITIVE

Just as there are some people who will sap your resolve and hinder your progress, so there are others who inspire and energise you. Who these people are will depend a lot on who you are, but it's my theory that they all have something in common. They have all discovered what it is that they are passionate about, and therefore what it is that they can excel at, and how they can go about this. It's nothing to do with talent or intelligence in the conventional sense.

Don't make the mistake that one of my clients made. He said that he struggled to absorb information because he wasn't a very fluent reader. But there are now so many other ways to access information. If you're someone who responds better to things that you hear, then go to podcasts and audio books to find out what you want to know. It's all about identifying your ideal learning style, which we'll look at more closely in Chapter 9.

SUMMARY

Your life experiences and your current perception of the world create your environment for you in a very personal way.

You are also subject to physical, mental and social factors in your environment to varying degrees.

The things you choose to watch, read and listen to have a powerful impact on your mental environment: choose them carefully.

The company you keep has a huge influence on you. If you can't change your friends and family, change the way you think about them and respond to them.

CHALLENGE

- Pick out three things that you have been reading, listening to, and watching (one each) that have a negative effect on you.
- What are you going to do to change this?
- Tweet me at @grenadejay and let me know your plans!

CHAPTER 4

LOOK, FEEL, THINK, DO

In the previous chapter I gave an overview of the various elements that go towards shaping our environment, and in this one I want to look more closely at some of these elements, starting off with diet, because this has such a huge impact on how we operate day to day, and on how we look.

Look

You are what you eat: it's as simple as that. If you are over-weight, it's because you are putting too much into your body, and if you are underweight, you're not putting enough in. This is common sense, but unfortunately not common prac-tice! If it were, we wouldn't have our current obesity crisis. To lose weight, you need to be in a caloric deficit.

That said, everybody's nutrition needs are different, and it's not for me, in a book, to be telling you exactly what you should and shouldn't be eating. There is no such thing as 'the perfect diet', no matter how much people who have found a particular diet that suits them evangelise about it. This is something you will have to work out for yourself, based on an honest appraisal of what – and when – you're eating.

Being honest with yourself is half the battle. A lot of people say to me, 'I don't eat much, but I'm still struggling to lose weight.' That may be true; perhaps they are not eating a lot in terms of quantity, but what they are eating has high calorific value. Take a doughnut, for example. A doughnut has around 500 calories – the same value as a proper meal of chicken and rice. The doughnut won't fill you up for long, leaving you ready for another 500 calories or more at the next meal time. Poor food choices are an important factor. You need to try to focus on your protein intake, because a high protein intake will satisfy you a lot more, making you feel less hungry. (And if you are in training, a higher protein intake will help to maintain muscle.)

And don't forget drink! Somehow liquids seem as though they must be very low in calories, but nothing could be further from the truth. A bottle of wine contains on average 700 calories. That's almost half the average female's calorie intake for a day. One glass of wine, on the other hand, can be easily accommodated into your calorie intake over a few days. If you're the sort of person who goes down to the pub and sinks eight pints, you need to be aware that it's going to take your body at least eight to ten hours to burn off the calories from those pints, and – because alcohol is a macronutrient and the first thing that your body burns off – that's before it's even started on the kebab that you had afterwards!

Timing is important, too. If you are not eating enough food during the day, you could well have an energy crash in the evening, which could leave you prone to overeating then. On the other hand, if you are someone who really can't face breakfast, it doesn't make sense to force yourself to eat it if you're only going to double up on these calories later on in the day.

So how to tackle all this? Again, writing it all down is the key to progress. I encourage my clients to spend a week being totally honest with themselves as they write a food diary. Not only do they need to log when and what they're eating, they also need to note down when they're hungry, when they're not hungry, when they're tired and when they're thirsty, to get a better picture of how their body works, and, perhaps even more significantly, of their habits, some of which they may not even have been aware.

This gives you an opportunity to harness some of those habits rather than try to change them. Remember, the less you try to change all in one go, the greater the chances of success. If you're somebody who doesn't eat a lot of food in the morning, and then tends to overeat in the evening, the diet to suit you might be an intermittent fasting diet, with a window for eating from 2pm to 8pm. The timing works within your habits and routines, and you simply will not be able to take on board an excessive number of calories during this time.

Below I've listed a few tips to help with making changes to the way you look, but when you add them to all the other little tweaks I'm suggesting in this chapter, they'll also help to lay down the foundation for adopting new habits.

LOOK

Understand what's really going on by starting a food diary.

Swap over to having bottles of beer rather than pints – that could save around 1000 calories on a Friday evening!

Consider vodka and tonic, which is less than 100kcal per drink.

Don't force yourself to eat at times when you're not hungry.

People don't eat so much when they're busy, so try to avoid letting yourself get hungry at times when you have nothing else to do but eat.

FEEL

Part of the reason that food can be such a problem for us is that we tend to have an emotional connection with it. It can make us feel fantastic – or it can make us feel terrible. We eat meals with our families to celebrate, and we often catch up with our friends by eating out with them. Or we might eat on our own when we're bored.

The choices and habits handed down from our parents can be very hard to break away from as well. We tend to view them as normal and carry them on as our own traditions. When I was younger my mum allowed me to go into the kitchen to make rock cakes or pizzas – on the one hand, not the healthiest of foods, but on the other hand it encouraged my interest in recipes and led to the passion I have now for creating healthier meals and treats. Luckily, I was also very interested in my father's home gym – and the extension to our bedtime we sometimes got which gave him a bit more time in his gym.

Once you start to eat better quality foods in the right quantities, you are in fact starting up a virtuous circle that generates a whole chain of rewards. You have more energy, so you feel more focused, because you feel more active now that you are lighter, you feel stronger, and you feel happier because you are starting to achieve your goals. It's really important to take the whole package into account, but unfortunately too many people focus on looking good at the expense of feeling good.

I speak from experience on this, believe me. When I'm competing in body-building championships, and get myself down to a very low level of body fat, I may look fantastic, but I feel terrible. People come up to me and say, 'I'd love to look like you', and I have to say to them, 'Yes, but you wouldn't want to feel like I do right now.'

BALANCE

This is why you should be aiming to balance looking good with feeling good. A lot of women come to me saying that they want well-defined abs. But I have to ask them to be realistic: the average woman has 30% body fat. For a woman to reduce her body fat enough to have visible abs would entail a dangerous degree of weight loss that could have consequences for her entire body.

Another point I can't emphasise enough is that how you feel about how you look often depends on the company you keep. If you're spending a lot of time in the gym surrounded by people who are in phenomenal shape your perception of what is normal is going to be a bit distorted. You need to be aware that this perception isn't shared by everybody. (To take a very obvious example: my wife can't stand it when I'm on stage, competing, in the best shape ever. She just hates that look, and the same goes for a lot of the women who comment on the pictures that I post on line, whereas the men think I look great.)

Balance is vital when it comes to nutrition. You need to focus on getting the right proportions of the macronutrients (the proteins, fats and carbs) and maintaining that calorie deficit, while also making sure that you're getting all the micronutrients (the vitamins and nutrients). If you can get 80% to 90% of your food from good quality sources that will contain the micronutrients, you can afford to be relaxed about a couple of ice creams or a couple of glasses of wine. In fact, this 10% or 20% of highly pleasurable intake may not be nourishing your body, but it's nonetheless providing important psychological nutrition. You're enjoying consuming it , and it's protecting you from the fatal 'all or nothing' view of the world, which dictates that the minute you let a crisp pass your lips you may as well give up on the whole enterprise and go off and binge.

CASE STUDY: UNHEALTHY WEIGHT LOSS

Most people now know that crash diets tend not to work, but there is little understanding of how dangerous that can be. A recent study described the case of a man who lost ten kilos over twelve weeks. Superficially, this was good news, but when he had a scan that analysed his fat levels, bone density and muscle mass, it was revealed that he had lost eight kilos in muscle mass, and only two kilos of fat. He had in fact been eating too little and exercising too much.

It is worth noting that it is vital not to lose muscle mass, especially when you get older, as you need a certain level of muscle mass to stay mobile and physically independent.

You also have to bear in mind what your body is used to. I can cope with my own quite demanding regime because I spent seven years in the army eating good quality food and training hard. You can't just go from complete couch potato to lean, mean machine in the blink of an eye. You need to build a solid foundation of diet and exercise before you really start pushing your body.

FEEL

Maintaining the right balance of nutrients will help you feel good and look good.

Don't have unrealistic expectations for yourself: there is no need for you to have the physique of a bodybuilder unless you are planning to make a career of it! Bodybuilders who have dieted to very low levels of body fat may look great but they feel terrible!

Allowing yourself that glass of wine or that ice cream makes you feel better and has a real psychological benefit.

Pace yourself: you'll get better results if you build up your level of exercise slowly.

THINK, DO

The paradox we have here is that a lot of people just want to find themselves doing the right thing without having to give it a great deal of thought, and in the other camp we have a lot of people who know the right things to do, and who think about them constantly, but can't actually bring themselves to do them.

JUST DO IT

But there is a lot you can do towards weight loss and fitness that actually needs very little thought or planning. Holding out for the perfect diet or exercise plan could be preventing you from doing something very simple like getting off the bus or train a stop earlier, and instantly adding to the number of calories you're burning every day.

If you find the prospect of a complicated gym routine a bit daunting, then perhaps a simple goal like 10,000 steps a day is more suitable for you. And these days there are plenty of clever devices that can tell you exactly how many calories you are burning when you do this. If you're taking 10,000 steps a day, that's the equivalent of walking five miles, and just doing that will burn an additional 400–500 calories a day. That, for a lot of people, is effort enough to not only lose weight but maintain weight loss as well.

I'm sure I don't need to tell you that a lot of it is down to will-power. The way I explain it to my clients is that your willpower is like your phone battery. You wake up in the morning and it's at 100%. As you go throughout the day it gets depleted. And when it gets depleted, the harder it is to say no to things. When you're tired, and you don't have much willpower, that's the time when you overeat.

Sleep is therefore very important. A lot of people don't get enough sleep or they have too much sleep. If someone currently getting nine hours of sleep a day got up an hour earlier they would be about 200–300 calories a day better off because they're moving for an additional hour every day.

So there are no excuses for not getting on with some simple changes, many of them easily incorporated into your present routine, that you can start right away and that will make a visible difference if you stick with them.

THINK IT THROUGH

So you're up and running, perhaps literally. Now's the time to look at how you can refine your approach, understand how you function and make progress, building on the quick wins you'll have had from getting moving.

Everyone is different, and to fine tune your approach you need to find out about how your body works and to think about how your daily routines affect that. You will have noticed how there are some lucky people who seem to be able to eat like a horse and never put on any weight. What's happening here is NEAT, otherwise known as Non-Exercise Activity Thermogenesis. Basically, these people are very fidgety: they tend to wander up and down when they're talking on the phone, when they're sitting down they're waggling a foot, and so on. Because they're always on the move, they're burning an extra 500-600 calories a day. You may not want to adopt a habit of hyperactivity, but there is a lesson in there that might be helpful.

CASE STUDY

One of my clients was a forty-two-year-old woman whom I was helping to prepare for a show. What I couldn't understand was that she was consuming the same number of calories a day as I was: around 2,600. Normally women burn off calories far more slowly than men, so it was a mystery to me how she was managing to bring her body fat down while eating so much. Then I realised that she was a beautician and she saw around twelve to fourteen clients every day. She was on her feet all day, doing back massages, bending, kneeling – and lifting weights as well, so she was moving around a lot more than I was.

Think	Do
Understand your patterns of eating, sleeping and moving.	Take action: start factoring a longer walk/taking the stairs instead of the lift into your day.
Pinpoint bad habits you may have taken for granted.	Get a pedometer so you can have the satisfaction of knowing you've done your 10,000 steps a day.
Identify your most productive and your most creative times of day.	Dance to your favourite tracks for a few minutes every day: good for the body and uplifting for the spirits!

Timing Is All

Just as your will power is stronger when you're not tired, your mind works differently at different times of day. You can take advantage of that to help you think things through and to solve problems, or to generate creative ideas.

Personally, my thinking time is early in the morning, at 5:30 – 6:30 am. It's good because that is when I have the least distraction in my day. If I have to plan or map anything out, I've allocated that time to be able to do it.

When it comes to having bright ideas, it's often at times when you're very relaxed that new and creative thoughts seem to drift into your head spontaneously. (This is where writing things down can serve you well, as you can capture these original ideas before they drift off again!) From a business point of view, this might be the sort of time that you could use productively to explore new possibilities for your business. For me, this creative time is before lunch, but it could perhaps be in the evening, when you're pleasantly tired, but not exhausted – and of course for many people it's when they're in the bath or shower.

And don't forget about how other people, your potential clients, your target audience, will be using their time. If you're using social media, lunchtimes and evenings will be the best time to reach out to them. They will probably be more open to your offer on a Friday afternoon than at any other time.

SUMMARY

By way of summary, I'm sharing with you my own high-level 'look, feel, think, do' quadrant, but only you can decide what to populate your own quadrant with.

look	**feel**
Keep track of calories	Listen to your body
Exercise regularly	Practise gratitude
Get enough rest/sleep	Care about others
Drink plenty of water	Be kind
think	**do**
Read 30 mins a day	Write down thoughts and actions
1 hour power walk daily	Be a man of your word
Journal thoughts weekly	Practise what you preach
Always ask questions	Set long and short term goals

The key idea is balance:

> Don't let the focus on looking good be at the expense of feeling good.

> Don't let thought crowd out action.

> Get the most out of doing by applying effective thinking to it.

CHALLENGE

- Have a look at your calorie intake and ask yourself how it's making you feel.

- Identify what things you're doing without thinking, or if there are things that you're thinking about but never get round to doing.

- Tweet me at @grenadejay to own up.

CHAPTER 5

MAPPING OUT YOUR MOTIVATIONS

I remember playing a lot of computer games when I was younger. I could play these computer games for hours on end without getting bored, and as I got older I wondered why that was. Fast forward to today, and you have a generation of adults addicted to the phone games, obsessed with planting trees and building farms on social media!

People seem to commit a lot of time to these things that don't necessarily get you any nearer to your goals, be they wealth, health or happiness. So wouldn't it be great if you could use whatever it is that gets you so addicted to these games to drive you on towards your health and fitness goals, and even your professional goals? Well, you're in for a treat, as I'm going to show you how to do that in this chapter.

What we're going to do in this chapter is to map out your motivators. We're going to talk about both internal and external motivators, starting with internal motivation.

INTERNAL MOTIVATION

In order to get people to keep playing a game, its creators have to understand what motivates them, and to do this, they use the RAMP model. RAMP stands for Relatedness, Autonomy, Mastery and Purpose, and you can use these for the 'gamification' of your health and fitness goals, as well as your business goals.

gamification

/ˌgeɪmɪfɪˈkeɪʃ(ə)n/

noun

. the application of typical elements of game playing (e.g. point scoring, competition with others, rules of play) to other areas of activity, typically as an online marketing technique to encourage engagement with a product or service. "gamification is exciting because it promises to make the hard stuff in life fun"

If you can make a game out of your goals, you will certainly be onto a winner, especially if you're enjoying the game you're playing.

Let's have a closer look at the separate elements of the RAMP model.

RELATEDNESS

This element of the RAMP model ties in with the points I made in Chapter 3 about the need to control your environment. The reason a lot of people do not find themselves motivated enough to follow or complete a plan of action is because they are not living in an environment that helps them to achieve their goals. The urge to belong is very strong, and this is where you can turn herd mentality to your advantage. When you surround yourself with like-minded people who want the same things as you do and are on the same journey as you, you all stand a much better chance of success, because you can all support one another.

The important thing is to join a community, and we have a huge advantage nowadays in that we don't necessarily have to move geographically to do so. If you come across a bunch of people at the gym who share your goals and are at the same stage as you are, great! But if not, there will be dozens of people out there somewhere and you will be able to find them with a few clicks of the mouse.

As a trainer, my focus in my gym is to bring together people who I know will be able to provide each other with mutual support and encouragement, but I also have a lot of online groups, so there will be people for you to reach out to wherever you are in the world.

The brilliant thing about social media is that it gives everyone a voice. Many people who might find it difficult to speak up in an actual group feel more confident to do so in a virtual group. It also dispels any notion that you are unique in the problem you have. The chances are there will be others out there who have also struggled with what you find difficult. And who knows, some of them might not live a million miles from you, so you could even factor in regular physical meetings alongside checking in daily or weekly with them online to discuss your progress and set yourself challenges.

CASE STUDY: SETTING UP THE GRENADE JAY ACADEMY

When I created a Facebook group called Grenade Jay Academy, within ten days I had 1,000 members. One of the ground rules was that everyone who joined had to submit a two-minute introduction video. For a lot of people, that was one of the scariest things they had ever been asked to do and it took them right out of their comfort zone. But because they knew that everyone who had already joined had done it, it automatically created solidarity, a fantastic community feeling.

Another rule is that there is to be no negativity in the group. You can get plenty of that outside, and it's not helpful, so there's no place for it in the group. There's also an expectation that you will contribute to the group: put into it as much as you get out of it in terms of sharing experiences and tips.

Then there are the daily themes: Motivation Monday, Training Tuesday, Wisdom Wednesday, Foodie Thursday, Free Stuff Friday, Skills Swap Saturday and Selfless Sunday. They encourage a more balanced approach to fitness and generate a wealth of tips and tricks to help people.

And of course I give all my groups challenges every week. Sometimes that could be about getting them to open up and tell the group about what they're having difficulties with, and this is when you can really see the truth of the saying, 'a problem shared is a problem halved.'

A good group usually has a good balance of people, and it may be that there are times when you come across someone who doesn't subscribe to the values of the group and who threatens to undermine the progress you are all making. In those circumstances you have no option but to ask that person to find a group more suited to their perspective on things.

AUTONOMY

We all like to make our own decisions in life. This is why, if someone else puts pressure on you to lose weight, you are far less likely to do it, or if you do give it a go, you are far less likely to stay the course.

Autonomy is very interesting from a marketing point of view. So many people focus on telling you what to do rather than on showing you what to do get results, but one thing I learnt a long time ago is that while people like to buy things, they don't like to have things sold to them. Some of the top marketers in the world are well aware of this, and this is what is at the heart of, say, Apple campaigns.

If you analyse an Apple advertisement, you will notice that they never mention the price, or even why you might like to buy the product. No, what they do is show you someone using the product and how their life is improved by having it. You then can't help imagining how much better your life would be if you had one too, and then of course you want to buy one. It's a great marketing strategy!

And this is exactly the approach I take online and in person with fitness. I show people my life day to day, and the results that I get from the regime I am following. This gets people interested not only in what I'm saying, but also what I'm selling. So I haven't told anyone to do anything, I've just demonstrated in what is in fact rather a low-key way the benefits of what I'm doing. It's the equivalent of the office colleague I mentioned in Chapter 3, who didn't tell anyone that they should be losing weight but simply got on with it himself until he found people starting to ask him for advice.

It's open to everyone to become a role model for someone. I tend to take little bits from a variety of people: my role model in a business context is Gary Vaynerchuk, and in terms of mindset and marketing I admire Seth Godin, Tim Ferris, Peter Sage, Simon Sinek and Robin Sharma. There are plenty of people, though, who have just one inspirational figure who is a real spur to them. When the going gets tough, they can ask themselves, 'What would X do?' and get a constructive answer. What you need to remember, though, is that even role models are human and you must accept that they are not perfect and may from time to time do something that you disapprove of, or at least question.

Finally, never forget that failure is an important part of autonomy. If you are out there, ploughing your own furrow, and genuinely responsible for your own actions, you will stumble sometimes. That's fine. That's how you learn. And if you look into the backgrounds of the people who are your role models, you'll find that they have all had failures in their past, but they've picked themselves up and pressed on.

MASTERY

Many people have the wrong idea about mastery. They think that there is a fixed end point to be reached, beyond which there is no further progress. This could not be further than the truth: there is always more to learn, a higher level to reach, and this is something that games designers have understood very well. Once you have reached one level in a game, a whole new challenge opens for you to reach the next level. This constant shifting of the goalposts is what maintains your internal motivation.

I've been going to the gym for eighteen years now and I never think 'OK, that's it. I'm done now.' It keeps me motivated to know that there is always another level to get to and that this will last me the rest of my life. The mistake that a lot of people make is to set a short-term goal and go at it, hell for leather. They end up with whiplash effect: they reach that goal, stop suddenly when they get to the top of that mountain, and realise that it's potentially downhill all the way from there – as opposed to looking around and saying 'Right, which is the next mountain to climb?'

There is no such thing as stasis, whatever the context. You don't just get to a certain level of happiness and stay that way, because things change all the time. And with wealth, we know that beyond a certain point, additional millions just don't make any difference. Mastery comes in different shapes and sizes: for some it's constantly striving to be better in their chosen field; for others, it is a desire to reach, say, the level of wealth that will enable them to go off and pursue their true passion, be it philanthropy, collecting art or travel.

With mastery comes the ability to teach others, and it gives the lie to the saying, 'Those who can, do, and those who can't, teach.' I think that what sometimes happens is that people don't realise how well they 'play the game', but once they do, they find that they want to share that with others, fire them up and get them good at it too. This is the challenge that lies beyond reaching the highest level of the game – whatever that 'game' is in your life.

PURPOSE

Why are you doing what you do in the first place? That is the most important question to ask yourself! Are you trying to lose weight so you can feel better, or because you want to have well-defined abs for the beach? Both of these could be good as short or long-term goals, but what happens when you achieve those goals?

As important as it is to have these goals, it's vital to have a long-term purpose. Mine is to keep myself healthy and fit enough to walk my daughter down the aisle – and her daughter as well. This lifelong purpose is going to take some commitment, because even when I achieve my short-er-term goals, I will still have a reason to keep working hard and consistently.

One of the positive effects of having a lifelong purpose is that it allows you to take a more measured approach to your goals, acknowledging that certain things are simply beyond your control. If unforeseen circumstances throw you off course, you have plenty of time to get back on track. It helps to mitigate that dangerous all-or-nothing mentality that sabotages so many people's efforts.

Having a purpose gives shape and meaning to your efforts. To look back and be able to see how you have progressed towards your purpose, demonstrating patience, perseverance and commitment, is far more satisfying than looking back on a rather random selection of unrelated activities.

EXTERNAL MOTIVATION

Everyone needs external motivators, be it a show, a 10k run, a wedding or a holiday. External motivators really do work. You're externally motivated to go to work because you're paid to go. In fact, a lot of people do their jobs because it pays the bills. They don't realise that if they changed the way they're externally motivated they could pay the bills and still do something they enjoy.

It's a question of finding a good balance. I found that my driving motivation doubled when the pressure was on me to build up my business for myself, as opposed to building things for other people. If you look at the example of painters, they are highly internally motivated to express themselves through their art, but once they receive a commission, they become less interested in painting, because it's no longer about what they want to do, it's about what someone else wants them to do.

It can be hard to distinguish between internal and external motivators, as some activities can function as both. If you take the concept of 'Relatedness' and of surrounding yourself with like-minded people, that's an internal motivator because it is that feeling of companionship and solidarity that is supporting you. But such a group is also capable of generating external motivators in the form of friendly competition.

CASE STUDY: THE POWER OF THE LEADER BOARD

At the moment I've got about fifteen friends in a particular fitness group, and we're competing to see who can do the most steps in a week. I was at the top of the leader board, with 110,000, but I've just added a friend who's got 115,000. In the grand scheme of things the leader board doesn't really matter, but the fact that I'm now only in second place and he's teasing me about it via the leader board app, is making me up my game. Yes – a leader board can be a fantastic motivator.

You can set up any number of external motivators based on what makes you tick, but here a couple more ideas have proved popular with people:

There are websites that enable you to put money in a pot and set weight loss goals. If you don't achieve those goals you lose your money. Meanwhile, everyone who has met their goals shares the money in the pot.

There are fitness watches and applications that enable you to compete against yourself, and to go for your personal best, but you can also add your friends into the app and measure yourself against how they're doing.

A lot of people try to keep quiet about their goals, in case they fail. Well that just makes it more likely that they will fail, because they have no external motivation to succeed. They are not holding themselves accountable or enabling anyone else to do so.

Commitment and accountability can be powerful external motivators, certainly for me. I'm anxious to be seen as a man of my word, so if I tell everyone what I'm aiming to do, it means I just have to make sure I fulfil that intention.

This is really important in the world of business, where visible accountability will build up trust in your business, and trust in your business is something that money simply can't buy. It is down to you, and whether you keep your word.

DON'T SET YOURSELF UP TO FAIL

Be realistic about what you are holding yourself accountable for. As with changing habits, if you hold yourself accountable for too many things, then you're destined for failure. Having one big mission statement and two smaller commitments that you know you can honour is a far more realistic proposition.

Don't set yourself unrealistic deadlines, either. I get a lot of emails from guys who say things along the lines of, 'I'm going on holiday in three weeks and I need to lose fifteen pounds.' Well, I'm sorry, but you should have started sooner. OK, you might be able to do it, but only through such an extreme diet that you will be miserable for the next three weeks and your body will be like a sponge while you're on holiday: within a week you will have regained the stone you shed, and then some. What's more, once the holiday is over, the external motivation will have gone.

You've got to look at longer-term external motivators, say six to seven months, and build in checkpoints along the way. Although a year for a weight loss goal might be a long time, three monthly checkpoints along the way give you a chance to see your progress and hopefully take heart from what you're achieving – much more satisfying than simply going from A to B.

SUMMARY

Surround yourself with like-minded people to reinforce your motivation.

You are responsible for your own progress, and you can set a powerful example if you choose to.

Your journey is never complete: there is always another level to progress to or another path to explore.

You need a lifelong purpose to give meaning and shape to your short-term goals.

Use external motivators to spur you on – be they money or competition with yourself or others – but use them wisely.

CHALLENGE

- Identify two internal motivators for yourself, using the RAMP model.

- Identify two external motivators, each with one checkpoint and one endpoint.

- Tweet me @grenadejay to tell me what you've committed to!

CHAPTER 6

WHAT GETS MEASURED GETS MANAGED

Experience has taught me that people are prone to focusing on the wrong things in their lives, and a lot of the time they are not even aware of it. The most obvious example of this is that they tend to spend a lot of the time watching box sets and playing games on their phones, yet they are adamant that they don't have the time to exercise and stay in shape.

However, this is part of the human condition and is known as a cognitive bias:

Cognitive bias

. A cognitive bias (e.g. Ariely, 2008) is a systematic (non-random) error in thinking, in the sense that a judgment deviates from what would be considered desirable from the perspective of accepted norms or correct in terms of formal logic. The application of heuristics is often associated with cognitive biases, some of which, such as those arising

> . from availability or representativeness, are 'cold' in the sense that they do not reflect a person's motivation and are instead the result of errors in information processing. Other cognitive biases, especially those that have a self-serving function (e.g. optimism bias), are more motivated. Finally, some biases, such as confirmation bias, can be motivated or unmotivated (Nickerson, 1998).
>
> . Behavioural Economics

I want to concentrate on the cognitive bias that I call the focusing effect, which is what happens when people place too much importance on one aspect of a situation, which makes it impossible for them to predict accurately what the consequence of their actions will be.

An extreme example of this effect is a fatal air crash that occurred because senior members of the crew were so fixated on a cockpit indicator that appeared to show a problem with their landing gear that they failed to register that the plane was running out of fuel.

The consequences may not be as drastic, but people do this all the time when it comes to their fitness and business goals: they concentrate too much on one particular issue when in the grand scheme of things it doesn't matter that much. I had one client who focused so much on what he should be eating after his workout that he completely overlooked what really mattered, which was the consistency of his overall nutrition on a daily basis.

A lot of clients complain to me that they can't lose or gain weight, but if I ask them how many calories they are consuming, they don't know. Once they start tracking and measuring their calories, they can see where they are going wrong. It's only once you start tracking your activities that you can see the reality rather than the assumptions, the bigger picture rather than the close-up of one detail, the patterns and habits that are holding you back.

THE CURSE OF 'BUSYNESS'

When I ask people how they are, their response is often, 'Busy'. When I ask them why they are so busy, and what exactly it is that they have to do, they often can't remember exactly what it is that has got them so tied up. This is usually because they have failed to plan: they haven't written these things down and allocated specific times for completing them.

When someone goes about their day knowing that they are busy, but with no plan of action for when and how to complete the things they need to do, it's no wonder that they are busy all the time, as nothing is ever really finished. I want to cover in more detail the topic that I touched on in Chapter 1: the importance of writing things down and mapping out your day, which will help you use your time a lot more effectively.

This also helps massively with procrastination, or displace-ment activity – call it what you like, but most of us are experts at finding things to do that are not what we're meant to be doing. I know it's one of my weak points: I have a bad habit of having lots of tabs open on my computer and lots of notifications on my phone, and then finding it very hard to concentrate. This is why I've come up with a plan of ATAC (pronounced 'attack'!):

 **A** NALYSE AND PLAN

 **T** IMETABLE

A CTION

C OMPARE

Let's work through these elements step by step, so that you can manage your workload and get the best out of every day.

ANALYSE AND PLAN

Proper analysis of what you want to achieve is vital for your success, and the information in Chapter 1 will help with your analysis. I can't remind people often enough that they need to establish what their problem *really* is, not what they *assume* it is.

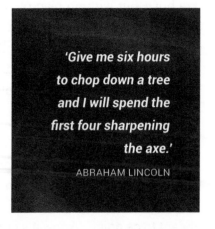

'*Give me six hours to chop down a tree and I will spend the first four sharpening the axe.*'

ABRAHAM LINCOLN

Establishing a base-line is also crucial: you won't be able to do any measuring or managing of your progress unless you know where you're starting from. It's all too easy to rush off and launch yourself into activity in a fit of enthusiasm, but you need to know, and record, your weight, your turnover, your speed – whatever it is – before you make any changes.

Next, think about having to fill up a jar with a number of stones of different sizes. It would make sense to put the big ones in first and let the little ones fill up the spaces in between them. If you start off by putting all the little ones in first, you may well find that there is no room left for the big ones, or that the big ones won't fit in completely. Well, it's exactly like that with the tasks that you have to complete in a day.

I recommend writing down the three most important tasks to be completed in your day. If you're struggling to identify which are the most important, ask yourself the following questions:

Have you a deadline to meet?

Is there a sequence of tasks that have to be done in the right order?

Which task is going to make the biggest impact?

Is it a task that will enable you to maintain consistency?

Is it a 'selfless' task?

From your list, schedule the most boring or unpleasant task first, to get it out of the way. If you leave it till the end of the day, there's a distinct possibility that it won't get done. These sorts of tasks tend to loom larger and larger, the longer they are left undone, but once you tackle them, you'll wonder what all the fuss was about. (Bear in mind the wise grandmother who told a child that if she didn't eat the cabbage on her plate the minute it was put in front of her, the portion would just grow bigger and bigger!)

In fact, this is a very constructive approach to life in general. If you spot a problem, nip it in the bud straight away, before it gets any worse, and don't assume that anybody else is going to take responsibility for it because they probably won't.

> '*Touch a thistle timidly and it pricks you, grasp it boldly and its spines crumble.*'
>
> WILLIAM S. HALSEY

CASE STUDY

When I start working with a new group of online clients – that's twenty or thirty strangers – the first thing that I ask them to do is post a short video about their particular problems and aspirations. On most of the courses it takes at least two days for someone to post a video, but once they've done that the others come in thick and fast – within about five hours. It seems as if everyone is just waiting for someone else to go first, worried perhaps that they are going to look stupid. In fact, everyone has great admiration for the brave person who made the first move and ends up being tremendously relieved to find out that others have the same problems that they do.

Now that you have your three tasks, and you know which one you're going to start with, make a realistic assessment of how long you need to complete them. It's usually safe to assume that things always take longer than you think they're going to, and it's always helpful if you've allowed some extra time to accommodate unforeseen problems – loss of internet connection and power outages are not unheard of!

TIMETABLE

The night before, map out the times that will suit you best to get those three tasks completed. It's really important to factor in some breaks (mental relaxation from tasks that you're focusing on can be very stimulating and creative), and also some activities that you will look forward to and enjoy (in my case, watching TV, reading and catching up with YouTube subscriptions).

As you can see from the diagram below, I have mapped out my day, starting off with the three main things that I need to get done today. Now all I need to do is fit the activities I want to do – be it recreation or relaxation or smaller tasks – around the big three.

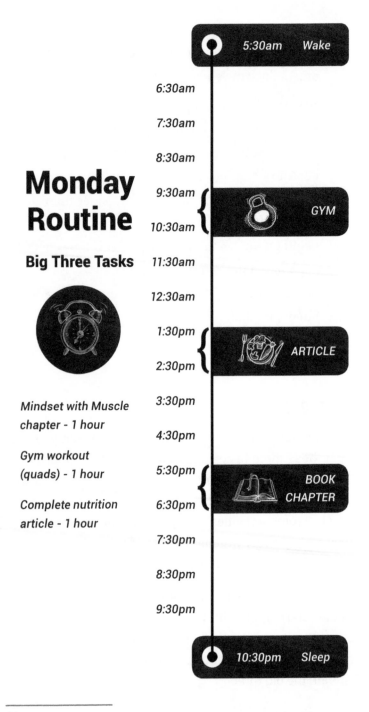

Monday Routine

Big Three Tasks

Mindset with Muscle
chapter - 1 hour

Gym workout
(quads) - 1 hour

Complete nutrition
article - 1 hour

5:30am   Wake

6:30am

7:30am

8:30am

9:30am

10:30am   GYM

11:30am

12:30am

1:30pm   ARTICLE

2:30pm

3:30pm

4:30pm

5:30pm   BOOK CHAPTER

6:30pm

7:30pm

8:30pm

9:30pm

10:30pm   Sleep

But a word of warning: just because you have written everything down and planned everything, it doesn't mean that it will all get done. Sometimes you can allocate time for a certain task, and no matter how hard you try to complete it, it just never seems to get done. This could be for a variety of reasons, and it's worth having a closer look not only at how much time you're allocating for activities, but also at when you're scheduling them.

CASE STUDY

I had a client who was struggling to keep to his training. He was always skipping sets of exercises and repetitions, and sometimes even missing the entire session.

What he had done was to schedule his training for his lunch break. He had an hour's lunch break. It took him about ten minutes to get to the gym and ten minutes to get back, which meant that he had only ten minutes to get changed and get dressed again, leaving him with only thirty minutes for his workout. He ended up so stressed that his time in the gym was completely unproductive, as he was doing a rush job to make sure he could get back to work on time.

We looked at alternative times for his work-out, and he decided that it was better for him to get up a little earlier and train before work. Just this switch in his timetable gave him plenty more time to train, and in fact fired him up no end for the day ahead, as he felt he had accomplished something while others were asleep.

Finally, don't make the mistake of pouring all your energy into analysing, planning and time-tabling, and failing to move on to the vitally important action bit! I worked with a client who was getting ready for a body-building show. I discovered that he had a mid-morning task sheet, a mid-afternoon task sheet, an evening gratitude sheet, and mind map, and so on, but he wasn't actually making that much progress with his physical preparation. Time to move on to the action bit!

ACTION

The action you are going to be taking is the culmination of your planning, so my message is, keep your planning simple, don't let it crowd out the time you have for action. It's all too easy to get carried away by making beautiful charts, etc., but these are only the means to an end. You need to decide what works for you, both in terms of your commitments, and of how you feel at different times of the day.

For example, while the received wisdom might be that early in the morning is a good time to meditate, it's probably not going to work for you if you are a night owl. A similarly quiet time at around midnight will be more productive. In terms of exercise, not everyone takes to early morning as my client in the case study above did. For some, hitting the gym after work is a good way to release tension and put away the cares of the day.

Also, as action is the point of all this, be prepared to be flexible – up to a point. If your goal is a fitness one, and you're finding that your workout is going very well on a particular day, then stick with it for an extra fifteen minutes and adjust your activities for the rest of the day accordingly. You are not a robot. When you're in the zone, you're in a kind of flow state, and the knock-on effect from the adrenaline rush you're getting will make you more productive for the rest of the day – by spending more time away from work you end up getting more work done!

This is where having planned out your day helps, because you will know exactly what's on the agenda for the rest of the day and how feasible it is to tweak it. (It would be fine to pinch fifteen minutes from your reading time, but not fine to make yourself fifteen minutes late for meeting a client, for example.) But I've said, 'up to a point,' because at the same time you must avoid making a habit of doing more of what you like doing at the expense of other things that have to be done.

Part of operating effectively is based on getting enough sleep, and this is another area where you need to know yourself and your needs. I'm a firm advocate of getting up an hour or two earlier to get things done, and to have some time for reflection before phones start ringing and emails pinging into your inbox, and this really works for me. But if you don't get enough sleep, you won't be able to focus and you will lack energy, so find your ideal balance. Too much sleep can make you as sluggish as too little.

Don't overlook some of the mundane tasks that don't feel as if they're contributing much to your grand plan, but create the conditions for you to work effectively. Activities like cleaning the house or weeding out your inbox come under this heading, because they are creating a clear environment that will help you to focus. If you then associate these activities with a reward (as discussed in Chapter 2), or combine them, where possible, with another activity, you will feel more motivated to do them. Here are some examples:

Cleaning and listening to an audio book/podcast: many mundane tasks don't demand your full attention, so take the opportunity to catch up on new information in your area of interest

Weeding out your inbox and listening to music: music can in fact help you to focus and complete a task quicker.

Catching up on your accounts while enjoying a cup of coffee.

COMPARE

Now that you've put so much effort into planning and time-tabling, and you're taking action, you need to be sure that it's the right action, and that it continues to be the right action. Monitoring your progress against your baseline will enable you to see how effective your action is.

How frequently you monitor will depend on what it is you are monitoring. Monitoring your weight on a daily basis can be deceptive. Comparing your weight on successive days is meaningless, because there are fluctuations in the amount of water your body is holding. What I recommend to my clients is that they weigh themselves every morning for a week and then calculate the average for that week. If they repeat this over successive weeks they can then compare the averages and get a much more realistic picture.

If your goal is a business-oriented one, you will obviously need to monitor over a longer timescale: months and quarters. You will also need to factor in all the external elements that may have a bearing on your business, be it weather, exchange rates, developments in your locality, etc.

Again, it makes sense to write this all down, to log it in whatever way suits you best, whether it's jotting it down in a notebook or creating charts and spreadsheets on the computer. Whatever makes comparison easy will work.

Once you can see your progress, you can identify where you need to put in more effort or do things differently. Obvious responses to lack of progress in weight loss will be increasing the amount of exercise/reducing calorie intake, and in business it might be approaching a new target audience. Whatever changes you make, you need to log them too, to see if they're having the desired effect.

The other element you need to factor in is feedback. It may not be measurable in such a precise fashion as weight, number of reps, etc., but you still need to keep in touch with it, and, certainly in a business context, to be responding to it, even, or perhaps especially, when what is being fed back is not to your liking.

It's clear, then, that ATAC is a circular process: once you have the data to monitor your progress and compare your present state with your previous one, you are in fact re-entering the analysis phase, and should be tweaking your plans according to your findings.

Remember, as Albert Einstein said,

> *'Insanity is doing the same things over and over
> again and expecting a different result'*

is absolutely true, and using the ATAC model will guard against that.

Summary

Focus on what is important, not what seems important.

Identify just what it is that you do with your time.

Plan your course of action.

Set a timetable for your day that ensures you will be able to achieve the three most important things on your agenda every day.

Just do it! Use the plan to guide action; don't get bogged down in planning.

Monitor your progress and make adjustments where needed.

CHALLENGE

- Draw up your own plan for the day, based on the ATAC model.
- Take a picture of it and tweet it to me @grenadejay.

CHAPTER 7

PASSION BREEDS SUCCESS

Something strange happens when I talk to people about nutrition, training and mindset: I completely lose track of time, especially if I am talking to someone who is equally passionate about those things. I end up deep in conversation, and I really enjoy interacting with them and finding out what they think. What's great, though, is that most of these people are my clients and they are paying me. Basically, I'm getting paid to do the things that I love.

Back when I was at school I could never have imagined that it would be like this. I never did very well there because I didn't enjoy it. It felt like a chore to learn, to read and to talk about things that I didn't really want to learn, read and talk about. Apart from anything else, it was very boring and I struggled to retain information about things that really didn't interest me at all.

Unfortunately, I believe that people are conditioned in this way from a very young age, and for many of them it simply doesn't work. They spend years in education doing subjects they're not interested in, to do jobs they don't really like, to pursue a career that they don't really want.

But if you find something that absorbs your attention completely, something that makes the time fly by without you noticing, then you've found your passion.

When your passion is your business, the entire game changes, and this has changed the way I think about success forever.

WHY FOLLOWING YOUR PASSION WILL BRING YOU MORE SUCCESS THAN A JOB

When I lost my job and finally started to follow my passions, I began to read more and learn more about the things that I wanted to do. And a funny thing happened... I started to absorb and remember the information that I was hearing and reading, simply because I was interested in it.

I started to implement what I was learning, as I was using it every day for work. To firmly establish in your brain what you have learnt, there is nothing like putting it immediately into practice – something you'll understand if you have ever had training on new software, but not actually started using it until some weeks or months later, by which time you will have forgotten everything that you've learnt.

In the past I had looked on education as something that was done to me. I went to school and teachers told me what to do and what to think about. Then I joined the army and had senior ranks telling me how to dress and where to go as well! I never spent much time seeking answers or wanting to become better educated for the sake of my career.

But when you are passionate about what you do for a living, you end up spending a lot of time on self-development, and you improve very quickly, because somehow you suck up the information like a sponge. In fact, what you're doing is developing a good habit without even noticing it – you're picking up routines and positive practices with no problem because the rewards are so worthwhile. It's a virtuous circle.

Passion Generates Creativity

Creativity never really came to me until I started doing what I wanted to do in life. Thinking outside the box was not something I had ever done or really been encouraged to do. I had always just listened and taken orders, and I would probably never have gone beyond that if I had not decided to follow my passions.

What happened when I started to follow those passions, however, was that I began to look at things in different ways. I asked myself how I could make fitness more fun and exciting for other people, and I started to 'think outside the box' in applying everything that I knew for the benefit of other people.

Looking back at how my business has developed, I realise I could never have predicted when I started that I would have a diverse range of services and packages to offer people, through such a varied range of media. It just goes to show how much focusing on what you enjoy stimulates ideas and a willingness to run with them.

Passion Gives You Energy

I've recently opened my own gym facility and I've been putting in some crazy hours! I was working six to seven days a week in the first few weeks, starting at 4.00 am and finishing at 9.00 pm, then forcing myself to head home and get some sleep before doing it all over again.

If I had been asked to work these hours in a normal job, I would have told the management to stick their request where the sun doesn't shine! The reality is that time just disappears when you are loving every minute of what you do, and it seems to give you an insane amount of energy. What to someone else would seem a rather punishing regime is something that I thrive on.

> '*Although we tend to believe that time flies when we're having a good time... studies indicate what it is about the enjoyable time that causes it to go by more quickly. It seems to be the goal pursuit or achievement-directed action we're engaged in that matters. Just being content or satisfied may not make time fly, but being excited or actively pursuing a desired object can.*'
>
> PHILIP GABLE, UNIVERSITY OF ALABAMA

I think many people have been conditioned to believe that there are only eight hours in a day. They are starting work at nine, finishing at five, and their approach is something along the lines of, 'I have an externally motivated work ethic based on getting paid every month, so once I've done my eight hours I'm off the hook and I can head home and forget about my job.' Once they're home, often the feet go up and the TV goes on.

I'm sorry, but if you've kissed your kids goodnight by 8.00 pm, you've still got another few hours in which you could be working before you go to bed, though unless you're running your own business you won't see things from this perspective.

So bearing in mind that the average person works eight hours a day – and much of that time might be spent procrastinating – it's not surprising that when passionate entrepreneurs put in sixteen hours a day of non-stop hustle they very quickly achieve their goals.

It's the energy that passion generates that will see you through the tough times. When I was made redundant, I didn't know what I was going to do, but as soon as I made the decision to follow my passion it was as if a bubble had formed around me. Suddenly I saw there were twenty-four hours in a day and I really only had to sleep for a few of them. I had this sense of being in control of my own destiny, and a deep conviction that things would work out OK. Passion was keeping me motivated through adversity: it enabled me to look at the positives in everything that I was doing and it eventually saw me come out on top. That really moulds you as a human being.

PASSION SELLS

I like to think I am a pretty good salesman! But this is only because I know that what I am selling can genuinely benefit each and every person who buys it. I spend hours and hours chewing people's ears off about my services, but as they are my passion, they are an easy sell rather than a hard sell, which increases my sales and grows my business. I get an immense amount of pleasure from seeing the look on people's faces when they realise that after so many years of trying they are finally getting the results they've been after. It's brilliant when you can combine your passion with making a real contribution to other people's lives.

But a lot of people struggle with their business as they are simply trying to sell a product because they need the money, not because they believe in the product. They're worried that someone is going to buy it and then discover that it's no good. When you talk about a product or service you are genuinely passionate about, it sounds the same whether you do it as part of your work, or outside of work, because it's something that you live and breathe. You will have an aura about you as you talk about it, your face will light up, and the person you are talking to will be able to see your conviction and your sincerity quite clearly, and will believe in what you have to offer. In my own case, it's perfectly clear that I've been taking my own medicine and that it works!

BUILDING YOUR BUSINESS

I think before you start developing a business you must be realistic with yourself. Too many people seem to imagine that they can apply their skills to anything, but there is more to it than that. You need to understand exactly what it is that you can offer, understand whether there is a need for it, and understand who would actually want to buy it. It's all very well to get excited about your business offer, but you have to be able to see it from the perspective of potential customers as well as from your own perspective. And potential customers can be far from rational when it comes to thinking about what they're looking for in a product.

Quite apart from the basic cost–benefit analysis people undertake when they're considering buying something, it's useful to analyse:

> people's fears – of disappointment, failure, hu-miliation (certainly in the context of fitness), of the unknown properties of what they are buying;

> ❯ people's frustrations with products or services that appear to promise a lot but do not deliver; and

> ❯ the differences and similarities between your product or service and everybody else's.

Think also about how you buy goods and services on line. Here's where analysis can provide insight rather than paralysis: go back over a recent transaction and try to identify your motivations and emotions at any given moment, and then apply the lessons to your own marketing.

STARTING OUT

To be honest, I was more or less forced into starting a business. I just thought, 'I'll jump straight in at the deep end and try to swim.' There wasn't a lot of strategy involved; I was just going to put my all into it and make it happen.

I was lucky enough to be able to get a significant amount of credit, so I rented some premises for a studio, and launched myself into it. It was trial and error, to begin with, just testing things out, and, most importantly, not giving up when things didn't seem to be working out. After all, I didn't want to lose my investment, and that was what motivated me to carry on. Everyone needs some incentive to make it work, some 'skin in the game', as they say, and mine was that in effect I had no 'skin' left so I just had to make it.

How much of a risk you can take will of course depend on your personal circumstances. A twenty-two-year old with no commitments is far better placed to work all hours and survive on a pittance than someone with a family to support, so timing is everything. It may be that you will need to tread water for a while until, say, your children can support themselves, but this nevertheless gives you an opportunity for learning and preparing for when you can launch your business, and once you do, there will be that much less on-the-the-job learning to do.

In this early phase the most important thing you can do is listen to people. Get as much feedback as you can from your customers and clients, in as many different ways as you can. A casual conversation can be far more useful, and enjoyable from a clients' point of view, than an impersonal survey. And try to find out what it is that people are not saying to your face, through social media and through your informal networks. My business model has changed hugely as a result of feedback, and of continuing to analyse and evaluate exactly what it is I'm doing, which I'll explore in the next section.

DEVELOPING THE BUSINESS

When I started my business about four years ago, it was very results-based, by which I mean that a client presented themselves to me looking a certain way, I would transform them, and they would end up looking different. That was how my mindset worked at that time. My job was basically to get them from 'before' to 'after' as quickly as possible. I gave them a plan of action, and if they followed it, they'd get a result. The only thing that they learnt from that was how to follow a plan of action. It didn't educate them about why the plan worked or inspire them. In fact, I gave the client the minimum, because I feared that if they knew exactly what I was doing, they would do it for themselves, and I wouldn't be needed any longer. But this changed at about the time that my focus shifted from myself to other people. As I became more focused on my wife, and on our baby daughter, who was about to be born, I also became more involved with my clients – and I actually put on about forty pounds! As I became more attuned to other people's needs, my business began to grow (as well as my waistline, temporarily).

My whole outlook became more abundant, and I saw my work as being to teach them everything I knew. Now not only can they understand how to effect that transformation themselves, they can sustain it as well. And guess what? They still need me because they enjoy spending time with me, and because they value the requirement to be accountable to me, to check in with me for some assurance; and they value the advice and encouragement. They need me because I will be honest with them in a way that others won't be. What this discovery brought home to me was the importance of sound values in business.

Business values

Always be honest with clients

Go for the generous approach: what more could you offer them?

Be open to feedback

Don't try to sell anyone anything you wouldn't be happy to buy yourself

Be yourself; don't pretend to be some fitness guru/ business tycoon/etc.

Make sure your customers'/clients' trust in you is never misplaced

Tackle problems as soon as you see them arising

Clients are your marketing material and that's why it's worth going beyond the call of duty for them. You may be advertising online and elsewhere, but that only gets clients in the door. After that, it's all down to the experience they have.

A client came up to me the first week after I'd opened the gym, when we'd been getting some good reviews. He said he'd been meaning to put a review up, but I told him to wait six months. I said, 'Well, we're a new business, and like any new business, we want to make a good impression, and so we're currently in our honeymoon period. I'll know I've done my job if you feel the same in six months' time as you do this week.'

Finally, don't undervalue your business. If you don't value it, why should anybody else? Membership of my gym is significantly more expensive than elsewhere, but that's because I offer a lot more than other gyms. You may have a cheap gym membership, but if you haven't made any progress over three years, it's actually rather expensive. You could come to my gym and sign up to a three-month transformation programme, which would in the end be far cheaper. This applies whatever the product or service: if you have put your passion into developing it, it will be a premium product that should carry a price that reflects the time, care and effort that has gone into it.

CREATING A TEAM

A few years ago, I heard something in a podcast that really changed the game for me. It was 'If you are the biggest asset in your business, then you don't have a business.' I realized that if you took me out of the equation, you would be left with absolutely nothing. I realized that I needed to create a team of like-minded people that I could mentor, coach and build up so that we could all sing from the same hymn sheet and support one another to grow the business. I'm in the middle of this process right now.

The fact that I now have a team of people with complementary skills and backgrounds has dramatically increased the appeal of the service that I offer. Everyone is different, and clients tend to gravitate naturally towards the team members whose style suits them. And I make sure that I give my team members plenty of autonomy because I know just how much I hated being micromanaged. I aimed to recruit 'intrapreneurs', not entrepreneurs – intrapreneurs are happy to grow their own business in my business, knowing that they still have that safety net. Then I let them loose to come up with their own ideas, as long as they are in line with the values of my business. I couldn't be happier when I see some of my old clients signing up with my new trainers, because I know that they'll continue to progress, and I'm proud to have created a team of people that my clients are willing to trust.

Summary

When your passion is your business, you will be motivated as never before. The hours devoted to developing your passion into a business will fly by.

Following your passion will stimulate your creativity in ways you could not have imagined.

Selling your product or service is easy when you have the conviction of your passion behind you.

Generosity in your approach to your clients will reap rewards. They will respond to your genuine desire to go the extra mile for them.

Ensure the health of your business by building up an enthusiastic team who share your values. Give them the freedom to come up with ideas and make their own way within the values of your business.

CHALLENGE

- What are you most passionate about? What could you talk about all day?

- How could you build that into a business?

- What would stop you?

- Tweet me your passions, your business ideas, and what's stopping you putting them into practice @grenadejay.

CHAPTER 8

FALLING IN LOVE WITH FAILURE

WHY DO PEOPLE FAIL?

In some ways, I think 'How do people fail?' would be a better question. As I see it, it's not so much failure or the prospect of failure that are the problem, it's how you react that really matters. I've identified three factors that amplify the setbacks we all encounter in life and make them so much worse.

THE BLAME GAME

It's all too easy to blame something or someone else when things go wrong. Someone fails, but rather than learn from that failure, they will point the finger and say, 'Well, it failed because of that person' or, 'It didn't work because of X or Y'. It's the kind of rationalisation that makes you feel better because it distances you from the situation. The problem with this approach is that you don't learn anything. If it's someone else's fault, it means that you don't take responsibility, so you don't have to make any effort to find out what went wrong and see if it can be put right. It means that you certainly won't undertake any of the analysis that I've emphasised the need for elsewhere in the book. What follows from this approach is that you either repeat the mistake (and we've already established that you can't keep doing the same thing and expecting a different result), or you abandon the whole project, which in effect sets the seal on your failure.

NOT INVESTING IN YOURSELF

Just deciding you want to do something is no guarantee that you will be able to achieve it. At the very least you need to invest the time to learn about what is it you are trying to do. You may already have the specialist knowledge behind your passion, but you won't necessarily have, say, the financial and marketing knowledge that you need to put your business on a sound footing and to get it known to prospective customers. Of course, there is masses of information out there, but that makes it even more important to be selective and not to adopt a sort of pick and mix approach to developing the skills you will need to build your business. If need be, take a course of some sort, pay for expert advice. This is all part of your commitment to your passion, and maintaining the necessary focus (remember 'Follow One Course Until Successful'?).

Building my business was no exception to this rule, and here are some of the ways I invested in myself during the development phase:

I paid for online courses and services from the best in the business so I could learn from their methods.

I spent time with people who were playing a bigger game than me and paid for their time so I could pick their brains.

I haven't been afraid of spending money on things that might not work; it's only by experimenting with different technologies, applications and platforms that you learn what works and what doesn't.

I've committed myself to reading two or three business books a month and spent time experimenting and applying the things that I have learnt.

Once I've invested in a certain method or strategy, I temporarily stop looking for alternatives until I've finished trialling what I've invested in.

I've invested in my social skills by doing things that are outside my comfort zone (such as meeting up with complete strangers for business lunches, which I organise at the last minute).

WORRYING ABOUT WHAT PEOPLE THINK

A lot of people allow themselves to be discouraged from following their passions by the negative opinions of others. They might have good ideas and start to make plans, but as soon as they announce them to others, they're met with a barrage of doubts and criticism: 'What if this happens? What if that happens?' But these critics are not the ones with the ideas and the passion. They are not the ones who have the motivation to persevere and to solve problems, so it's not surprising that they see nothing but obstacles to a chosen course of action. Nevertheless, by pouring cold water on people's plans, they manage to sow seeds of doubt and generate enough fear to put people off trying to achieve anything.

HOW IS FAILURE RELATED TO FEAR?

Fear and failure work very closely together, and go a long way to explaining why people don't achieve the things that they want to achieve in life. Fear, as defined by the Oxford

English Dictionary, is 'an unpleasant emotion caused by the threat of danger, pain, or harm'.

The purpose of fear is to protect you, to promote your survival. In extreme circumstances your brain activates your body into a flight or fight response to prepare you for what may be about to happen. The key words here are 'about to happen' – it's all about anticipation.

Fear protected our distant ancestors from being eaten by predators. However, as we are unlikely to be pounced on at any moment by a sabre-toothed tiger, our fears are more usually related to things like what other people think of us, how we would cope with a reduction in income, or perhaps more generalised issues such as climate change. None of this requires us to be in the adrenaline-fuelled survival mode we sometimes find ourselves in.

Interestingly, babies are born with only two fears: fear of falling and fear of loud noises. All other fears are fears that we learn because of our culture, and they can in fact vary considerably from one country to another. People in Japan, for example, have a far greater fear of 'losing face' than we do in the West, and I know from my travels in Africa that the way of life that many take for granted there would fill us with fear – of disease, of hunger, of having to cope without what we see as the basic amenities of life.

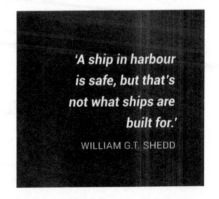

'A ship in harbour is safe, but that's not what ships are built for.'

WILLIAM G.T. SHEDD

So in reality most of us, most of the time, have very little to fear, and yet we let fear of imaginary harm inhibit our activities and our quest for success.

Fear of failure looms large in our society, and some would say that it starts far too early. The jury is out on whether the extent of testing used in schools is improving standards or producing a generation of children afraid to fail. The fact remains that most people are fearful of following their passions because of the risk of failure. What I hope to demonstrate is that failure need not be something to fear; it can be helpful, constructive – creative even.

WHY SHOULD YOU EMBRACE FAILURE?

There is one word that I'd like to see firmly attached to failure: experience. There is no substitute for experience when it comes to learning and developing. If people don't try new things because they are afraid of failure, they are missing out on huge opportunities, not the least the opportunity of finding their true potential.

When you go to the gym and you push yourself to the point of failure, you find out where your limits are. Next time you'll know where that limit is, and therefore how much more it is reasonable to push yourself to go beyond that. And that's how you progress. You wouldn't have been able to identify your starting point for improvement if you hadn't persevered until the point of failure. So the best way to look at failure is as feedback!

Suppose you failed at lifting a weight. There could be a number of reasons for this:

You weren't strong enough to lift it.

You didn't have enough energy to lift it.

You weren't using the correct technique.

What you need to do now is find out which of these was the cause of the failure and work specifically on that problem before you try to lift the weight again. If you know you were using the correct technique, you'll either need to develop your strength further, or think about why you didn't have enough energy on that particular occasion and adjust the timing of your workout, or perhaps your nutrition. How much more constructive is that than simply accepting your failure by telling yourself that you're just too much of a weakling?

There is a very valuable lesson about what distinguishes failure from failing that I learnt from a guest who I've had on my podcast, Jay Samit:

'There is a huge difference between failure and failing. Failing is trying something that you learn doesn't work. Failure is throwing in the towel and giving up. True success comes from failing repeatedly and as quickly as possible, before your cash or your willpower gives out.'

This links us back directly to the ATAC model in Chapter 6, specifically to the 'analyse' and 'compare' parts of the cycle. When you fail at something, you need to examine how far your achievement is from your expectations and analyse that difference. Again, the tendency to view things as either black or white can lead people to throw out the baby with the bath water. A more reasoned assessment might show that, far from failing outright, you have actually achieved a partial success.

If a meticulous analysis of why you have failed, or not achieved as much as you hoped, reveals a number of possible causes, you need to be rigorous in the way you tackle them. Take the simple example of a missed weight loss goal: tempting though it may be to go off and alter your diet, change your exercise regime and spend longer in the gym, it will not get you to the heart of why you missed that goal. What you actually need to do is just change one thing at a time, give it a chance to work, and then measure its impact. That's the only way you will be able to isolate what it is that is causing the problem or having the biggest impact.

This is in fact the scientific method. Scientists do not consider themselves as failing every time something doesn't turn out as they hope it will. They call their process experimentation, and progress emerges through trial and error. It will, for example, take many hundreds of formulations before medical researchers create a vaccine that will tackle a disease safely and effectively. (In this context it's worth noting that Jonas Salk worked sixteen hours a day, seven days a week for more than two years to develop the polio vaccine.)

People like Jonas Salk are the acknowledged experts in their fields precisely because they have made all the mistakes there are to make and learnt from them. There is a tendency to mistrust experts these days, and people often complain about, say, the plumber who turns up and fixes something in about ten minutes by turning a valve or some such, and then charges £80. What they're forgetting is that they're not just paying for that ten minutes. They're paying for several years of apprenticeship, followed by more years

'Even if you fall on your face, you're still moving forward.'

VIKTOR KIAM,
CEO OF REMINGTON

of confronting every plumbing problem under the sun, and developing skills, knowledge and experience on the job.

You can apply these principles to anything. Push yourself out of your comfort zone and don't worry about failing (though do show some regard for the health and safety of others!). If you fail, take the time to examine what went wrong, or what could have gone better, and identify what you can do to fix it or improve on it next time.

This approach to failure is what builds experience. Prestigious employers often prefer to hire someone who has made mistakes because they know that they have been prepared to take a risk, and that they will have learnt from their mistakes. (They're not so keen on people who make the same mistake twice!) I hope I've demonstrated that, all in all, failure is nothing to fear.

TAKE A SHORT CUT

There is another option, and that is to let others make the mistakes for you. But so that you don't miss out on the lessons and benefits from making mistakes, you need to choose the area in which you let others make the mistakes carefully.

The weightlifting failure I set out earlier in the chapter offers a good example of where you could take a short cut to improving your performance. If you identify that where you're going wrong is in your technique, then it makes sense to seek out an expert and get advice from them rather than risk working your way through further poor – and possibly dangerous – techniques.

WHEN FAILURE IS THE FOUNDATION FOR SUCCESS

There are countless stories that spring to mind to demonstrate how people have battled through their failures to ultimate success. At the heart of all these stories is someone who didn't give up, but soldiered on through the tough times till they achieved their goal, as these famous examples show.

Mindset models	Early failure	Ultimate success
J.K. Rowling	• Failed marriage and extreme poverty • Rejection by 12 publishers	• Numerous literary awards • 400 million books sold • Net worth of $1bn
Michael Jordan	• Rejected for varsity basketball team for being too short	• Olympic gold medallist • NBA player of the year many times and numerous other sporting awards • Net worth of $1.14bn
Shaun Pulfrey	• Tangle Teezer brush rejected by 'dragons' on Dragons' Den	• His business now worth £200m • Product exported to 60 countries • 13 Tangle Teezers sold every minute

Failure didn't deter these people from keeping on trying, which just goes to show that you can use failure as a spur. One of the mistakes that people often make in fitness terms is to think that once you've achieved your body transformation you can just stop. But this is the beginning, not the end, and lasting success comes from moving the goalposts as you go along, so there's always a degree of failure to overcome. The cure for yo-yo dieting is to have long-term goals that succeed in embedding good habits. Successful businesses do exactly the same when they innovate, aiming to boost sales by launching new products and services, and opening new markets.

I came across one of the most remarkable examples of this tenacious approach when I attended a public speaking course. The organisers had three of their top public speakers there to demonstrate their skills. They all told us that they had originally been acutely nervous and couldn't speak in public at all, yet now they are getting paid as professional speakers. When I asked one of them what had changed, he said to me that he was still nervous, but he had learnt how to face it, and although it required constant effort, what drove him was the opportunity to succeed at it daily and the knowledge that he is getting paid to do something he never thought possible.

This approach also gives you the opportunity to reshape the narrative of failure into something that can serve as encouragement for yourself and testimonial for your clients. One of the biggest assets a person or a business can have is integrity. People actually like to hear of individual or business failures as long as these stories include an ending that tells them how you were able to remedy the failures.

CASE STUDY

You could day that my very first Mindset with Muscle podcast was a bit of a failure! I recorded the entire thing in stereo instead of mono, which meant that some people couldn't hear the guest (but it still shot to No. 1 in an iTunes chart). As soon as I noticed my mistake, I made a point of telling everyone about it, and about what I'd learnt from it:

> Don't record a podcast in stereo.

> Nothing is perfect; getting the information out there is the most important thing (progress over perfection).

> Success comes from pushing yourself beyond your comfort zone (two weeks before I didn't have a clue about how to record a podcast, let alone publish it).

Looked at through the prism of a series of obstacles overcome as you get fitter and stronger, your fitness regime is a developing success story. In the context of business, honesty about your failures and how you have overcome them is far more persuasive than a narrative of being born with a silver spoon in your mouth or having some sort of mysterious Midas touch.

SUMMARY

Don't court failure by letting others undermine you and undervaluing yourself. You don't know what you're capable of until you try.

Don't let fear hold you back: most fears are more imagined than real.

Learn to use failure as feedback for learning and development; this is what research scientists do every day.

Make failure a springboard for achievement, just as some of the most successful people in the world today have done.

CHALLENGE

- Identify three things that fear of failure has stopped you achieving.
- Tweet those three things to me @grenadejay.

CHAPTER 9

KNOWLEDGE ISN'T POWER

The title of this chapter is actually a bit misleading, because of course knowledge *is* power, and without knowing anything it becomes very hard to do anything. But as human beings we have a problem, and that's that a lot of the time we know perfectly well what to do but we don't do it.

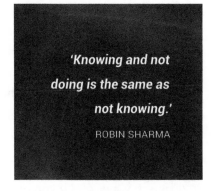

'Knowing and not doing is the same as not knowing.'

ROBIN SHARMA

Knowing by itself is not enough. We know very well that if we eat too many calories we'll put on weight; we know that if we drink too much, we'll wake up with a headache; and we know that if we smoke we are risking lung disease – yet many people carry on doing all these things. In a more general sense, we know that if we don't push ourselves to do the things we are scared of, we will always be scared of them.

Applying your knowledge is one of the most powerful things you can do when it comes to succeeding with your goals, but you'd be amazed at the number of clients I have who have been to the same seminars as me and read the same books as me, and yet have done nothing with the information they gained. Listening to a motivational speaker or reading a book on productivity will not by themselves make you more motivated or productive. This is why I'm going to focus in this last chapter on a seamless process that will take you from acquiring the knowledge you need quickly and easily through to putting it into practice, so that you can start getting the benefit from it.

SOAK UP KNOWLEDGE

You can absorb information a lot more quickly if it's information that's related to a subject you are passionate about. In the previous chapter we looked at how passion breeds success. Obviously, you will be far more motivated to read for longer and to dig more deeply in your research when it comes to topics that interest you, but there is an effect beyond this that means you take in the information much more readily, and you retain it better over the long term as well.

It's helpful to understand that people absorb knowledge in different ways, and if you can identify your own learning style, it will make it that much easier to acquire and remember knowledge.

Learning is a sensory experience, and most people favour one of the styles describes below, though obviously not to the exclusion of all others:

Visual: you respond best to what you can see, so you prefer to learn from books and magazines, YouTube videos and seminars.

Auditory: you respond best to what you can hear, so you favour audio books, lectures and podcasts.

Kinesthetic: you respond best to what you can touch, so you prefer hands-on workshops and opportunities for practical training.

The learning pyramid below develops this a bit further. It may have been criticised for a lack of accuracy when it comes to the percentages of how much you retain, but it's still a useful representation of the options for acquiring and retaining knowledge.

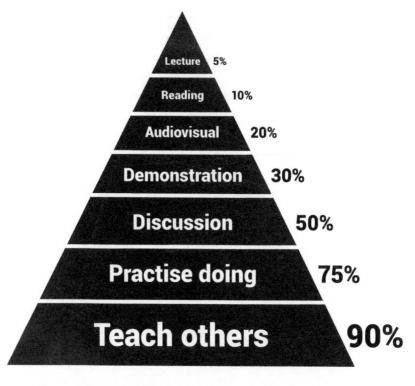

Lecture 5%

Reading 10%

Audiovisual 20%

Demonstration 30%

Discussion 50%

Practise doing 75%

Teach others 90%

The Learning Pyramid, National Training Laboratories, Betel, Maine

Although you might need to take the exact percentages in this diagram with a pinch of salt, as so much depends on personal learning styles, it still has some useful insights to offer about ways in which to go about learning and, just as importantly, consolidating what you've learnt.

Think back to the things you can still remember from school or college: how was that information delivered to you? Is there any information you have picked up recently that made a particular impression on you? Do you find yourself thinking about films you have seen or recalling books that you have read? Reflecting on these things may give you a few clues on how you learn best, or you could go to one of the many online tests for learning styles. Once you've identified what style of learning suits you best, you'll be able to go about acquiring knowledge more effectively, saving a lot of time and covering a lot more ground than if you are struggling with a learning style that doesn't reflect your needs.

RETAIN KNOWLEDGE

I have designed my own step-by-step process for retaining all the information you have acquired, especially information you have gathered from books. The acronym for it is CARAT, which neatly reflects how valuable your golden nuggets of information are!

C OMMIT — Commit to the same period of time for learning every day. This could be 30 minutes to an hour, and will be all part of building positive habits.

A BSORB — Find the learning style that suits you best: Books? Podcasts? Videos? Practical workshops?

R EFLECT — Think about how the information you are absorbing relates to you. It's OK if you don't understand it all, or if some of it doesn't seem to apply to you.

A PPLY — Put the information into practice as soon as you can, while it's still fresh in your mind.

T EACH — Speak to others about what you've learnt. If you are able to articulate something you've learnt and pass it on to someone else, you will find that this is information you'll never forget.

Let's look at each stage in the process more closely.

COMMIT

As with any type of learning, you need to build up the habit of acquiring knowledge. We learn best when we are exposed to knowledge about a particular subject regularly, and we're able to progress from simpler concepts to harder ones, building up familiarity with the topic as we go along. It is much easier if you commit time to this as a conscious action. Block a space in your diary every day during which you are going to acquire knowledge. For me this is usually at six in the morning, when I listen to an audio book or a podcast during my morning power walk. The early morning is quiet and uninterrupted, so it's the perfect time to listen and learn. At seven, when I watch a YouTube video for fifteen minutes while I'm having my breakfast, it's my time to get fired up for the day ahead, so it's usually a motivational video. At 3.00pm, I sit down and read one chapter of a self-development or business book for thirty minutes, which helps to stave off a mid-afternoon slump and inspires me to get more done.

Doing this means you'll be able to choose a time that fits in with your schedule, and that hopefully offers some space and quiet in which to learn. Committing to this time also sends your brain a signal that now is the time to learn and helps with shutting out distractions.

The time in between these regular sessions is time that your brain spends subconsciously processing what you have learnt. Trying to cram in too much all in one go can be counterproductive.

And if you've committed this time, the next part of the process should be that much easier.

ABSORB

The word 'absorb' represents an action that takes place over a period of time. It's not a word like 'flash' or 'thud', where the action happens in an instant. This is why you need a specific time commitment. Absorption can only happen if your brain has the space to open up and focus on the matter in hand.

For the most efficient soaking up of knowledge to happen, you need to be practicing the learning style that suits you best. It's a waste of effort if you are struggling to concentrate on a podcast, when actually you would find it all much clearer if you were looking at a video, or reading something up from a book.

Don't underestimate how effective it can be to reinforce knowledge by going over it again, perhaps in another format. This is especially true of complex subjects, where following up a podcast with a YouTube video may make everything clearer, not least because by the time you come to the video, some of the material will be familiar.

REFLECT

You can also reinforce what you have absorbed by reflecting on it afterwards. This will be a lot more productive than simply 'swallowing' large chunks of information and thinking 'job done'. And this reflection shouldn't just be idle musings about what you've just learnt, it should be a considered assessment of how what you've just learnt is relevant to you and your situation.

A lot of books and podcasts contain stories about individuals who have followed a particular course of action, because we respond well to narrative. We have an innate understanding of the structure of stories, which usually start with a problem, follow the struggle to tackle the problem, and arrive at a resolution. We appreciate that actions have consequences and we expect to see those consequences played out in the stories. But not everything in any given story will be relevant to you, so you need to exercise a bit of discernment to identify what it is that chimes with your own story or contains a message for you.

If you look at how the iPod was marketed when it first came out, the whole campaign was about stories. People weren't being sold a sleek piece of kit that contained the ultimate in nanotechnology, they were being sold a narrative of what life could be like if they owned this device. What they remembered from the advertising was how they visualised their own lives would be after they'd made this purchase. It's said that Steve Jobs was inspired to take this approach by seeing what the story boarders produced once Pixar – originally a high-tech computer animation company rather than a film company – began work on *Toy Story.*

To help with your reflection, I would advise you to take the time to write down the things that you've drawn from your learning. You'd be amazed how quickly these insights vanish if you don't write them down. In fact, if you want to get the most out of your reflection, I would advise keeping a journal. It will provide you with both an instant reference for your learning, and a record of your progress. One of the many rewards of learning is being able to look back over the journey you've taken and seeing the strides you've made.

APPLY

This is the crucial step. Committing, absorbing and reflecting have laid the foundations for the moment when you can start to use everything that you've learnt and take action. If you have been through these stages, you can be confident that these actions will be well thought through and targeted at your objective.

But speed is of the essence; strike while the iron is hot; and other similar sayings. I'm sure everyone can think of examples in their own lives where they have got a new piece of equipment, or planned to become involved in a new sport, say, and read up about it, but then didn't do anything about for a while. The knowledge faded and with it the impetus to take action. (In this connection, the piece of kitchen equipment most notorious for being bought but never used is apparently a pasta maker.)

If you are serious about your fitness, or your business, take action straightaway, however inexpert, wobbly or amateur it may be at this stage, because when you've done it once, it becomes so much easier to do it a second and a third time.

TEACH

As soon as I learn anything new, I love talking about it to my trainers, or discussing it on social media. I find this is a fantastic way to get to grips with what a writer or presenter has been saying, and to filter it through my own perception.

You will know that there is nothing like having to explain something to someone else – how to play a game, perhaps, or how to operate a piece of equipment – for clarifying in your own mind how that game or gizmo works, even though you thought you had understood it perfectly. What tends to happen is that you automatically build patterns and short cuts in your mind without realising it, and it's only when you have to articulate a method or a process for someone else that you examine and unpack these patterns.

There are many ways of doing this, including new media opportunities that simply weren't available previously. You could:

> summarise what you've learnt in a blog;

> tweet about it;

> make a short video for YouTube; or

> ❯ simply have a chat about it with a friend over coffee.

Whether the statistic of 90% for retention of information from teaching is accurate or not, there's no denying that this bottom layer of the learning pyramid represents the most effective way of holding on to the knowledge you have acquired.

KNOWLEDGE INTO ACTION

To help with taking that first crucial step, I've come up with a very basic plan of action for you to draw up in response to the searching questions below, which you just have to follow through. What could be easier than that? There is plenty of scope for you to tweak it to match your area of interest, your commitments and your learning style, but I hope it gives you the momentum to get started, and to feel a sense of progress – your journey is underway.

Let's assume you have committed time to your area of interest, and you have indeed absorbed the information through some means. What next?

What have you learnt and how is it relevant to you? (Write it down!) → What are your plans for applying this information this week? → How will you get this across to others? - blog post?

Although I've represented this as a linear process, there is a sense in which this, too, comes full circle. In Chapter 5 we looked at commitment and the importance of keeping your word as important motivators to help you persevere. You will have demonstrated commitment in keeping your appointment with yourself to learn and following up on it, but in telling others about what you have learnt, you will also be demonstrating that commitment publicly and setting up the expectation in them that you are serious about what you are undertaking, which will help to keep you motivated.

And a final word of encouragement to get you started: don't forget the other powerful motivator we looked at in previous chapters. Reward! However daunting that first step might be, if you have something pleasurable to look forward to on the other side of it, you are far more likely to take the plunge. You could even build the reward into the 'Teach' bit of the model by feeding back to your friends over a coffee or a drink. It makes the whole prospect of learning much more appealing than the model we are used to from school or the workplace.

SUMMARY

Knowledge is valuable – but it can only be powerful if you act on it. There's no point in being an armchair expert in your chosen field.

Create the ideal conditions for learning by committing time and space for it, and make the most of these conditions by adopting the learning style most suitable for you.

Not everything that you read, see or hear will apply to you, even in your area of interest. Make sure you identify what is relevant to you and how you can use it.

Reinforce your learning by applying it straight away, and by relaying your learning to others.

CHALLENGE

- Using the CARAT model, see how much faster you can absorb and retain information.

- Tweet me @grenadejay to tell me something you've learnt, or how CARAT worked for you.

CONCLUSION

Now it's down to you. Only you have the power to make the choice to change your life, and to translate that choice into action. My role is to give you the impetus – and the tools – to take that crucial first step, and to guide you in taking the next one and the ones after that, through my tried-and-tested method for changing and strengthening your mindset to provide the foundation for achieving what you've set your heart on.

I hope you'll agree that, far from being some miracle cure, what I've set out in the book is a sound and well-thought-out course of action that takes account of the realities of life and doesn't expect you to be superhuman. Looking back over the chapters, quite a few rather old-school sayings came to mind:

> Nothing ventured, nothing gained.

> Look before you leap.

> Don't run before you can walk.

> Don't throw the baby out with the bath water.

There's proof, if you needed it, that the advice in these pages is based on wide experience of human nature!

So what *Mindset with Muscle* is offering is a very practical scheme, starting with an in-depth understanding of your particular problem and proceeding through incremental and manageable steps towards your goal. It also shows you how to ensure that your motivation is supported along your journey by peers, by rewards, by your own learning, and by your awareness of your progress – all the while keeping a sense of perspective and acknowledging your pre-existing commitments to family, friends and work. The book also offers you the unique opportunity to build in external support and accountability right from the start by sharing your goals with me via Twitter.

The fact that I've completed this book demonstrates to me that my approach works. The analysis and planning I've promoted throughout the book have helped me to combine writing it with the challenge of launching my new gym, and creating and managing a dedicated team of trainers – while not completely ignoring my family and friends. The learning I've undertaken has given me a strong framework for setting up a stable, popular and successful business. I could not have foreseen any of this at the point when I found myself unexpectedly unemployed!

Back to you: now's the time to make that choice to take action, to go for your goals. The plan is here for you to follow, and you can always visit me at grenade-fit.com. Don't forget that whether you need understanding advice or someone on your case, I'm only a tweet away.

Acknowledgements

My first acknowledgement has to go to my good friend Dan Meredith. Dan is a one of a kind human being and is the epitome of setting himself a goal and achieving it. He recently wrote a book of similar size to this in just seven days!

It was this commitment to his goal that made me realise I should stop dragging my heels and get this book written and done, so thank you, Dan.

The rest of my acknowledgements go to my wife Anna and my daughter Elyza. Without my wife's support for what I do I would not achieve half as much; and my daughter's birth has given me the added drive and motivation that I have now. I'm excited at the prospect of my daughter reading this book when she is old enough to understand how important it is to reach for the stars. Elyza I love you with all my heart.

And my final acknowledgment goes out to everyone who follows and interacts with me on social media. It's you guys and girls out there that drive me to do these crazy things and enable me to live a life that I never dreamed I could, a few years ago.

About the Author

Jamie Alderton is a fitness entrepreneur and professional fitness model and Director of GrenadeFIT Gym. This is a revolutionary training facility dedicated to transforming clients through nutrition, training and mindset.

After leaving the British Army in December 2009, Jamie's focus on self-development and self-improvement took him on a rollercoaster journey through physical and mental transformation.

In 2010, Jamie won the Musclemania British Novice Natural Bodybuilding title and after an eighteen month break from stage he returned to win the WBFF European Muscle Model Championship and a professional status.

In 2012, after being made redundant, Jamie's concentrated not only on his body but his business and brain too. Within four years he went from a tiny personal training studio and a maxed out credit card to one of the biggest personalities in the fitness industry with one of the best training facilities in the UK.

Jamie puts this all down to what he has learnt through experience and his main aim in life now is showing others how they can use these experiences to achieve massive levels of success.

To find out more about GrenadeFIT click on his website:
www.grenade-fit.com

Contact Jamie through:
Facebook – www.facebook.com/grenadejay
Instagram – www.instagram.com/grenadejay
Twitter – www.twitter.com/grenadejay